How to Pass Exams

Other books by Fred Orr

Conquering Shyness
How to Succeed at Part-time Study
How to Succeed at Work
Study Skills for Successful Students

How to Pass Exams

Second Edition

Fred Orr

ALLEN&UNWIN

First published in 1997
This edition published in 2004

Copyright © Fred Orr 1997

Allen & Unwin
83 Alexander Street
Crows Nest NSW 2065
Australia
Phone   (61 2) 8425 0100
Fax   (61 2) 9906 2218
Email: info@allenandunwin.com
Web: www.allenandunwin.com

National Library of Australia
Cataloguing-in-Publication entry:
Orr, Fred.
    How to pass exams

    2nd ed.
    ISBN 1 74114 551 1.

    1. Examinations - Study guides. 2. Study skills. I. Title.

371.30281

Set in 10.5/12 pt Garamond by DOCUPRO, Sydney
Printed by SRM Production Services, SDN, BHD, Malaysia

10 9 8 7 6 5 4 3 2 1

Cartoons by Peter Meldrum

This book is dedicated to my three children: Matthew, Vanessa and Katharine.
May they approach all the tests in their lives with mental clarity, a confident spirit, and with competence in skills.

Contents

Appendix   **132**

Preface

Examinations, in all of their varied forms, affect all of you at least once during your lives. Your secondary school years present your first exposure to major examinations, but the formal assessment process unfortunately does not end there. Even after leaving school, many of you will confront other types of examinations, such as employment interviews (actually oral examinations) and motor vehicle driver's tests.

Over the past many years at the Counselling Service at the University of New South Wales, I have seen large numbers of people with many and varied problems associated with examinations. Their concerns ranged from sleep problems before exams, to memory blocks and muscle cramping during exams. Some have also wanted to discuss fractured relationships which have occurred during the examination period. One of the most common issues is how to manage time, the eternal enemy of most students.

As jobs continue to be scarce and the competition keen, the pressure upon you rises. Unless you perform very well in an examination you might not get the job you prefer. Thus, preparing thoroughly and performing well in examinations are critical to your future success.

How can your preparation and performance in an exam be improved? For a start, read this book. The book has two major parts: Part I discusses preparation strategies for use prior to your exams; and Part II deals with performance aspects, such as controlling exam nerves, organising your revision and performing in the exam room. Some strategies and skills, such as training your mind to relax on command, will take several months to develop, so be sure to get started early in the academic year. If, however, your exams start in a week or two, you still might benefit from reading the final few chapters, which include the time-honoured tradition of 'cramming'.

The book is based upon well-established cognitive–behavioural principles which can help you to improve your preparation and performance. But first you must get started—and the earlier, the better. The first message of this book is *get organised*! Readers will soon discover the second major message—*keep working* on a regular basis. Having learned the fundamental lessons at the core of this book, you will want to know how these principles can be put into action. Read on.

You will probably benefit by first reading the contents and noting those chapters which have immediate importance and relevance. As will be discussed later, becoming more efficient when time is limited is a critical skill. So, go first to the chapters which address your specific needs. Learn the skills which will enhance your examination success and, as time permits and circumstances warrant, deal with the other chapters and issues at a later time.

A few words about the results of examinations and their effects upon your motivation. If you have had mainly successful experiences with examinations and you are reading this book to improve still further, well and good.

On the other hand, if your examination experiences have been less positive, read and learn from this book and then *actively* apply the principles at every opportunity. Every application will be a learning experience and a boost to your motivation. The more of these experiences you can have, the better your results are likely to become.

At this point, I wish you happy reading of the book and very good luck with all your examinations (however, don't depend upon this good luck—get started *now* on positive preparation).

Fred Orr
Sydney

Part I

Preparation for exams

1

Get organised!

'I spend so much time trying to organise myself, I don't have enough time to study.' — Frantic student

Some students try to organise their time too much; others avoid the activity altogether; and a few get totally confused by the process. As exams draw nearer, time for study becomes critical. Passing your exams can be a function of how well you manage your time. Complete the following checklist to see how you rate on time management skills.

Time and study checklist
- [ ] I can waste hours, and sometimes whole days, doing unimportant things.
- [ ] I study in a disorganised fashion.
- [ ] I find it difficult to separate the major points from the trivia.
- [ ] I revise too late for large exams.
- [ ] I often start study tasks, but do not finish them.

- ☐ I am plagued by indecision.
- ☐ I often repeat work unnecessarily.
- ☐ Instead of studying, I ponder reasons for failing.
- ☐ I can't sit still at my study place.
- ☐ I generally reorganise my desk top at the start of study sessions.

If you ticked more than five of the above items, then you need help in managing your study time. You may know of the common commercial adage, 'Time is money'. The academic equivalent is, 'Time is marks'. If you manage your time better, you will almost certainly get better results.

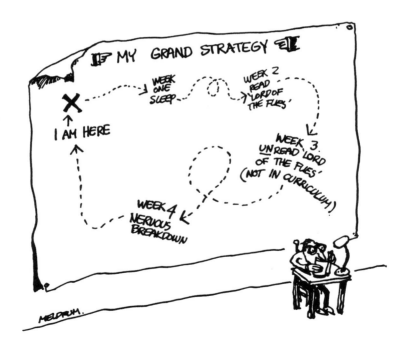

LONG-TERM PLANNING

How long is long term? The most appropriate time span here would be five to ten years, the time before you pursue your career goals in the work world. That might seem like light years away now, but having some idea of where your education is leading you can help you to manage your time better.

BRIAN—FUTURE VET

Brian had always related well to animals and decided in his early high school years that he was going to be a vet. In year 10, he spent two work experience weeks with different vets in his district. He found the work and long hours to be demanding, but he persisted with his plans. At university he joined the Veterinary Students Association, which held professional meetings and social functions. At one meeting, a country vet spoke about his large-animal practice. Brian approached him after the talk and discussed the possibility of spending some time at the practice during the summer months. The vet was receptive and the working visit was arranged.

How do these career-related experiences help with time management during the academic year? Brian was clear about his vocational goals, an unusual situation for most students. He knew very well that he needed the background of biochemistry, physiology and other demanding basic sciences. He found it easier to get motivated with a specific vocational view of his future. He planned his study sessions, putting the very difficult subjects first, as he knew they would be important to his professional work.

Even at a very early stage—say, high school years 8, 9 and 10—clarifying your career goals can be a significant help. You don't have to sign a contract committing you to any selected job area. At this stage, it's just a general guide to where you might be going. If you don't have a clue about what you want to do, try completing the following 3 × 3 exercise.

---

3 x 3 EXERCISE TO CLARIFY YOUR CAREER

1 I am good at the following three skills: (a), (b), (c).
2 My close friends would say that I am good at the following three things: (d), (e), (f).
3 In my spare time, I prefer to do one of the following three activities: (g), (h), (i).

You might wish to list more than three items in each of the three categories. Throw modesty aside and give yourself credit for your skills, abilities and interests. The better you know yourself, the better planner you are likely to be. Having completed the exercise, see if you can identify any trends suggested by the answers. Discuss your responses with a close friend or family member to see if they can offer any career suggestions. You may be very tired of being asked by your parents and their friends, 'What are you going to be?' but persevere.

You might wish to discuss the careers clarification exercise with a counsellor or careers adviser. Your aim is to get an answer to the question, 'Where is my study program taking me?'. Your career goals will be discussed again in the next chapter, 'Motivate yourself!', but now let's turn to semester planning.

SEMESTER PLAN

Whether you are in high school, technical college or at university, your academic year will be divided into terms, sessions or semesters (for convenience, let's use the semester). You will need to have a plan to guide your assignment preparation and exam revision for each semester of study. You might think that planning for end of semester exams in the first week of the semester is bordering on paranoia. Definitely not. In fact, exam experts say that the exam period begins on the first day of the semester. Any thought of exams might make you feel a bit uncomfortable, but unfortunately they are an academic reality and must be faced. At exam time, you will be responsible for the notes, readings, class activities, labs, field trips and any other academic exercises from the first day of the semester onwards. So, the sooner you plan for your exams, the better you are likely to perform.

One common student mistake is spending too much time on assignments during the semester and devoting too little time to exam revision. Students argue that their assignments are more immediate and demand attention—the exams are further down the track and less urgent. Urgency aside, you should really plan to spend preparation time in proportion to the total amount of marks which your various activities will earn—that is, put your time where the marks are.

For example, in Subject A, if you are assigned three essays worth 10 per cent each, two tests worth 15 per cent each, and one final exam worth 40 per cent, then you should devote your preparation time in proportion to the worth of each of these events. How can you work this out? Use a 'Semester-at-a-glance chart' (see page 8).

You can see that a fourteen-week semester has been charted and that four subjects—A, B, C and D—have been listed in the left-hand column. Adjust the chart to your present semester schedule. Having set up your chart, now place in the relevant boxes all mark-earning activities: quizzes, tests, essays, lab reports, class presentations, exams and any other assessments. Add to the chart any further assessments as you go through your present semester.

With all the relevant information charted, the next step is to record the preparation time for each event. You can

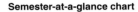

Semester-at-a-glance chart

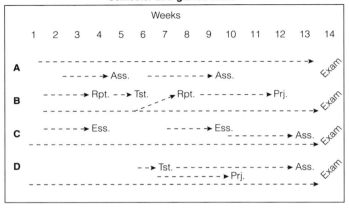

Key   Tst = test, Ass = assignment, Rpt = report, Prj = project

do this by drawing a dotted arrow representing the amount of time you believe is needed for thorough preparation. For example, you might have only a very short arrow leading up to a quiz, but you might want to place a long arrow extending across the entire fourteen weeks for your final exam. That long arrow might seem too long, but that's the ideal. I highly recommend that you 'learn as you go' from week 1 onwards and revise each week for your finals.

Your chart may now look quite complicated. Don't worry—this is the norm, as most students have too much to do and not enough time to do it all.

Look at week 7, a period which might seem to be relatively quiet as there is only one test scheduled. But, looking down through the column, you see eight dotted lines in addition to the test. Those dotted lines represent preparation activities for assessable events coming up in the future. Considering these preparation tasks, week 7 does not seem so quiet after all. With this work load, you will recognise the academic value of the Boy Scout motto, 'Always be prepared'.

Thorough preparation is the solution to good results. Inadequate preparation the night before is a pathway to panic and poor results. Think ahead and organise your preparation. No matter what type of exam you will be facing, you need to know your notes and other study materials very well. Revising stacks of notes takes time—generally much more time than is available during the two or three weeks before a major exam. As suggested earlier, assignments are often due in the final few weeks of semester and many students are more concerned about assignment completion than exam revision.

Rather than cramming too much activity into these final few weeks, prepare for your exams over the long term, right from week one. That way, there is no last minute panic and pressure. Revise the general concepts and themes for your final exams in a relaxed and confident state.

One additional point in planning your semester chart—include any time-consuming social activities, such as a weekend away. Losing a weekend just before a week in which three assignments are due could be disastrous. Place the important social event on your semester chart and then plan to finish the assignments beforehand. That could mean some late nights over the preceding two weeks, but you will enjoy yourself more knowing that your academic work is complete.

You might wish to make a copy of your semester chart so that you have one on the wall in front of your desk and the other in your notebook. Update the charts regularly so you have a clear picture of your current and future work loads. The general messages conveyed by the charts are: start early and revise regularly. Look ahead and note the assessments and assignments due in the next two weeks. Use this information when planning your time and work each day.

ELECTRONIC DIARIES AND COMPUTER PLANNERS

The electronic age has been with us for some time and many students now use electronic diaries or computer planners. Electronic diaries are slightly larger than hand-size and are programmed to accept dates, times and events which you enter into the diary's memory. Many of these diaries have alarm functions; address, telephone and fax memories; birthday reminders and other useful functions. Most have the facility for downloading information onto your computer at home.

There are several major problems with these very handy devices, the foremost being that they are frequently lost or stolen. A stolen personal planner can place the owner at organisational risk, especially if the information has not been downloaded at home. You may also be at risk if your home address and other personal details are retrievable by the thief. Be certain to take appropriate safeguards if you use an electronic diary.

Most computer shops will be able to recommend a variety of software planners for your home computer. These programs have all the functions of the electronic diaries and many more. You do have to spend some time keying in the data, but you will benefit in the future. Talk with any friends who are familiar with various personal planner programs and ask their advice. Visit your local software shop and see the programs in action. Once you have decided upon a time planner and personal organiser, read the user's manual and then key in the relevant information straight away. You will save heaps of time and energy and your results may well improve as well.

ORGANISING YOUR DAYS, EACH DAY

Whether you use electronic gear or pen and paper, you need to organise today and tomorrow—very critical periods of time! By making these days efficient and effective, you establish a success path for the rest of the week and further on.

The most important planning goals for any student are mapping out times to prepare for all mark-earning activities. Plan your days and weeks so that you have plenty of preparation time for your assessments. You will also need to budget for reading, research, note-taking and other study maintenance activities. It might seem that you will have no free time, but try to squeeze in your social functions and any other commitments. Study dates are one way to mix some *disciplined* work and social life, but mental control is necessary.

Most students will say, 'I think about what I want to do each day, but I rarely write these goals down'. Does just thinking about your study goals work as well as a written 'To do' list? Definitely not. There is a clear agreement among personal planning experts: *written goals are attained far more often than mental goals*. Perhaps the written goals convert the diary sheet into a personal contract. Whatever the reason, writing down your goals works—trying to keep them in your head works less well.

Some might ask: 'Why go to the bother of writing down study tasks and other things you want to do?' The simple answer is that you are likely to perform better in your studies and on your exams. There are other non-academic advantages as well. Just imagine what would happen if you remembered your mother's birthday three days late or you failed to pay a critical bill on time. These little things do matter and unfortunately they are often overlooked, especially during chaotic times. In order to avoid these embarrassing situations, what can you do? Plan every day.

Constructing an efficient daily plan involves more than just scribbling a few notes on a scrap of paper. The best way to proceed is to use a diary and devote one page per day. There are three important elements in an effective daily plan:

1 a precise description of each task to be done;
2 a priority ranking, taking into account task importance and urgency; and
3 an estimate of the time needed for task completion.

A fourth element is very important—a tick symbolising *done*! You might use a large red felt-tipped pen to record your ticks—and do so with gusto! Let's look at a sample daily plan.

Daily plan

Tasks	Priority	Time	Done (✓)
Plan Engl essay	1	60"	
Read Hist ch 5	2	60"	
Plan Chem lab	1	15"	
Revise Unit 14, Compt'g	1	30"	
TV Docmt'y, Biol	2	30"	
Call Peter, film Fri	3	10"	
Jog	2	30"	

Your daily plan will help you to organise your time and tasks. Be certain to use SMART tasks: *Specific, Measurable, Achievable, Relevant* and *Timed*.

There is absolutely no sense in setting goals which are too large or too complicated. You only stand to fail—and that will not boost your confidence. Your moods will differ each day, so adjust your approach. If you're feeling great, then tackle that very difficult essay. If your mind is foggy and your energy is low, then start with a much easier task, like transferring your chemistry lab figures to the data tables. The essence of good planning is high efficiency—use your energy and your time to best advantage.

KEY POINTS IN MAKING YOUR DAILY PLAN WORK

- Make a plan every day—preferably in a diary.
- Be precise in defining your tasks.
- Specify a time length for each task—very important when telephoning friends.
- Tick each task immediately upon completion—enjoy the feeling of accomplishment.
- Allow plenty of preparation time for long or complicated assignments.
- Plan for the weekends as well as week days, especially during the final weeks of the semester.
- Plan for short spurts of revision, especially during waiting times—use flash cards (see chapter 4).
- Use travel time for study—be sure to take your notes, books or other study materials.
- When planning tomorrow, look ahead two weeks and include preparation time for major projects.
- Remember to schedule revision for final exams well before the end of semester.

Caution—watch out for your friends. Even though you have constructed a very efficient plan for the day, your friends can lure you away from your desk. They can often present tempting diversions when the pressure is high. Say, 'No!' tactfully but strongly to friends who try to tempt you from your books. They will understand even though they might grumble. You gain more study time and very likely more marks by saying 'No!' Save the partying until you have more time available and then really enjoy yourself, knowing that you have earned a good break.

ORGANISING MAJOR ASSIGNMENTS

Preparing major essays and projects will be an important part of your study routine. These large assignments will take lots of time and it's best that the time be spread across several weeks. Let's look at a sample project—say, a 3000 word essay due in four weeks.

In order to estimate the time needed to complete this essay, some 'guess-timates' are necessary:

- Your library research, reading and note-taking might take about ten hours.
- For convenience, let's say the average essay paragraph is about 100 words, making the assignment about 30 paragraphs long.
- To be on the safe side, you might give yourself about 30 minutes to initially draft each paragraph, thus taking about fifteen hours.
- As good writing is good rewriting, give yourself another ten hours for several redrafts.
- Having completed the writing, you may need about five hours to prepare the final draft, with bibliography, footnoting, typing, binding and photocopying.

Your time plan should look like this:

Essay preparation time plan

Task	Time
Reading, research and note-taking	10 h
Initial drafting	15 h
Redrafting	10 h
Final drafting, photocopying, binding	5 h
Total preparation time	*40 h*

The above time allocations are estimates, but it is clear that preparing the 3000 word essay is best done over the four week period and *not crammed* into the final few days. This is especially true if you are currently working on more than one major assignment. When preparing your week's work, allocate time to the essay preparation functions. As creative writing often requires a quiet setting, you will need to plan carefully so that you have the time and conditions available. The most challenging part will be the initial drafting, so don't back away from the difficulties and leave yourself with an impossible task in the final week.

FREQUENTLY ASKED QUESTIONS (FAQ) ABOUT STUDYING

1. How much time should I spend studying each week?

This is probably one of the most common concerns of students (and their parents, if the students live at home). Unfortunately, there is no easy answer. Studying is really a very individual activity. The quality and quantity of studying varies with your subjects, your skills and your position in the academic year.

As an example, let's say that you are starting out in the first semester of your first year in an Arts degree. You have enrolled in four subjects—English, political science, French and psychology. You have fifteen contact class hours each week, including the language lab for French and the lab in psychology. You have weekly quizzes scheduled for French and nine essays or reports due during the fourteen-week semester. You will have six exams at the end of the semester.

What do these facts and figures mean when weekly study is considered? Basically, a lot of work. Putting your fifteen contact class hours onto a weekly planner might give the false impression that you have lots of spare time. However, if you plot the quizzes, essays, reports and exams onto a semester plan as suggested earlier in this chapter, the lead up arrows will show you just how busy you will be.

If you want a quantitative estimate of study time per week, plan to spend about one and a half to three hours in outside study for every class contact hour. That means organising about 22 to 45 hours for studying each week, plus the fifteen hours of class contact time. That could mean up to 60 hours of studying—much more than most full-time jobs. If it is necessary for you to work in a part-time job as well, be careful about committing too many hours, as your studying should be your first priority. Many students fail because they work too many hours in their jobs and neglect their studies.

Studying for up to 60 hours per week may seem as likely as jumping over the moon to some students, but it is important to emphasise that serious study at above passing level is going to require a lot of work. That is the reality of the matter. To do less is taking a big gamble.

2. Should my study approach differ from subject to subject?

Yes. For example, in mathematics, you will be studying processes, whereas in English you will be studying concepts. The mathematical processes are best learned by practising solving problems—many of them. Ultimately, you should be able to look at the problems on the exam and recognise the basic problem types. Then you should be able to use the necessary procedures for solving the problems. Certainly, you should practise with the exercise problems in your textbook. Read the theory section, then work through the sample problems. When you understand the theory and can see how it is applied in the sample problems, then turn to the problems at the end of the chapter. Work through these problems and if you experience difficulties, seek help. As you will appreciate, studying mathematics takes lots of time and much practise.

Studying English will be very different—not much problem solving, but lots of reading and writing instead. In most Arts and social science subjects, the reading list will be long. Your classes might involve discussions of the major ideas and concepts taken from the readings. In your exams, you will be expected to have a thorough knowledge of the central ideas and be able to write essays which demonstrate your abilities of critical analysis.

The physical and biological sciences can be a blend of the two study approaches used in mathematics and social science and Arts subjects. You will need skills in solving various types of problems, but you will also be expected to write essays analysing the major ideas.

Generally, it will be necessary to customise your study approach to your subjects. Take into account your interests, study strengths and weaknesses, and certainly your time. Be sure that you keep up to date with each subject and that you allow plenty of time for practice problems. Try to slot your most difficult subjects into your peak performance times each day. Do your easy subjects at other times.

3. Can I become a better essay writer?

Yes, but lots of practice will be necessary. One of the major problems with essay writing is that students do not take time to practise. They gamble on being able to perform at better than passing level on exam day. How many athletes would ignore regular training and hope that they can produce a winning performance at the championships? Very few—and these are the ones who are likely to finish last.

You can practise your essay-writing skills by arranging to submit regular mini-essays (about 250 words) to a teacher or senior student who is competent in correcting your writing. Arrange to submit two mini-essays a week for as many weeks as necessary to improve your skills. Collect your edited essays and take the corrections into account when writing your next one. The feedback on these practice essays is critical—you learn from your errors but they do not affect your grades. Each mini-essay should not take more than two hours to prepare. Your marker should be able to provide the red pen feedback in less than ten minutes per essay. Most students show a marked increase in their skills after only several weeks of writing these mini-essays.

SUMMARY

Planning your time and organising your study activities will win you higher marks. Be sure to revise each week and practise your essay writing and mathematics skills for best results.

2

Motivate yourself!

'Bodies at rest tend to stay at rest . . . ' — Inertia
'Is panic really necessary to get me moving?' — Student practising inertia

Motivation. You've heard the word many times and in many different situations. If you think it's something to do with getting into action, you're absolutely right. In fact, the word comes from the Latin word, *moveo*—to move. Applied to your major goal of studying and passing exams, motivation is all about getting to your desk and into your books and notes. Most of the action is going to be mental, unless you're studying applied physical education or some other action-oriented course. In order to see how motivated you are about your studies, complete the following checklist.

Motivation checklist

☐ I can't get away from the TV set or the Internet.
☐ Sitting down at my desk is the last place I want to be.

☐ Once at my desk, I tend to daydream rather than get into my work.
☐ I don't like the thought of having to study.
☐ My mind gets distracted too easily, especially when trying to study.
☐ Telephone calls are a pleasant distraction.
☐ I put off starting major projects until the last few days.
☐ I see little reason in having to study for so long.
☐ I get too restless when sitting at my desk.
☐ Fearing failure is just about the only thing which gets me moving on my studies.

Most of you will have ticked at least several of the items in the checklist. If you ticked almost all the items, you are in need of help to get you into action. Let's look at Leslie, who had major motivation problems.

LESLIE—NO MOTIVATION, NO FUTURE

Leslie was a final year high school student who was totally lacking in motivation. Her parents had discussed her poor performance with her teachers, but none could offer any solution to her motivation problem. Both of Leslie's parents were professional people who hoped that she would find some goal to stimulate her interest, but nothing seemed to work, including Leslie.

The motivation problem started at the beginning of year 11. Leslie was bright enough to get away with persistent procrastination. She made last-minute efforts—often starting her assignments the night before they were due.

However, as the workload became more intense and the subject matter more difficult, these last-minute efforts were less and less effective. In fact, she started to fail and prospects of university entrance were becoming dimmer. The school counsellor tried to help, but Leslie did not want to be seen attending the counsellor's office. Therefore her parents sought help outside the school.

Leslie was initially reluctant to come to see a counsellor, but she knew that unless something jolted her into action, she would continue to spiral downwards and most likely fail in her final year. We talked about her work problems, negative attitudes and general stagnation. The one major theme which kept surfacing was confusion about where her life was heading: 'I don't know where I'm going and what's more, I certainly don't know how to get there!' She seemed to think that in her final year of high school she had to decide upon a specific career and commit her life to that goal. Making such a major decision made her feel very anxious, and one way of coping was to withdraw from her studies. TV became the focus of her evenings and her books never left her bag.

Through counselling, Leslie gradually gained an understanding of her predicament. She also realised that most careers are the result of a series of steps, often taken in a zig-zag fashion, with the person learning more about themself and their career prospects at each step. She gradually accepted that she did not have to decide upon one area of work, but that she did have to begin to organise some options.

Once Leslie felt the pressure lifting, she became more comfortable about trying to apply herself to her studies. She finished year 12 with good grades and gained admission to the university of her choice.

MOTIVATING METHODS

Motivation problems are common, but also very challenging. As with Leslie's situation, breaking through stagnation requires some personal insight which is much easier to gain with the help of a counsellor. With more understanding of yourself, you are then ready to get back into action. But what types of activities can help to maintain your momentum? Here are some suggestions.

Keep a daily diary of goals set and accomplished

Ticking off tasks 'Done!' will make you feel better and perhaps project you into more action. One important note, however—make your tasks SMART ones, as mentioned in chapter 1.

S—Be *specific* when defining your tasks.
M—Make your tasks *measurable* so that you know how much progress you're making.
A—Be certain that your tasks are *achievable*.
R—Set *relevant* tasks for yourself.
T—Make every study goal a *timed* task.

Setting SMART goals for yourself and seeing them ticked off in your diary will make you feel good. You're making progress and getting ahead. Allow this positive feeling to spread into all parts of your life: home relations, study, employment, peer friendships, sport and recreational activities, and any other areas in which you are involved.

Plan pleasant events and special treats each day

Being stuck in a pit of low motivation is no fun at all. You know you should be out there doing something, anything, but you only get deeper and deeper into pessimism, inactivity and depression. How do you break out of this negative situation? There are no magical solutions, but you can experience some improvement by planning some pleasant events and special treats for yourself every day.

What qualifies as a pleasant event or a special treat? That will vary with each person. You know what you really enjoy. When you are in a positive mood, sit down and make a list of the activities, foods, places, people or situations which make you feel good. A Pleasant Events Schedule with 320 items has been used in the psychology profession for many years (no author can be identified at this stage). A random extract of ten items includes: dancing; sitting in the sun; riding a motorcycle; just sitting and thinking; social drinking; seeing good things happen to family or friends; going to a fair, carnival, circus, zoo or amusement park; talking about philosophy or religion; planning or organising something; and having a milkshake.

You can see from the list that the activities are quite varied. Some activities may appeal to you while others may seem quite uninteresting or even distasteful. The list serves as a stimulus for people who have been plagued by low motivation and physical/mental stagnation. The object is to help individuals low in motivation to get up and get going. The best way to prompt this movement is to provide suggestions of positive activities which might then induce further activity.

Make up your own list and then schedule at least one or two positive events/activities every day. Knowing that you have a pleasant event scheduled later in the morning will help you to get out of bed and into the day. Think of the pleasant event as a reward for having accomplished several work tasks both during the morning and in the afternoon. If you respond to this system positively, set some pleasant events for the evening so that you have three potentially productive periods on most days. Your life will become both more interesting and more effective because of these periodic rewards for ongoing effort.

Clarify your career goals

Just as Leslie was having difficulty motivating herself when she was uncertain about her career goals, the same can happen to you. It helps knowing where all your hard work is taking you. But how do you predict the future when your present situation is very confused? Crystal balls and fortune tellers are not very reliable, so seek some better source of information.

If you are interested in several different types of employment, attend careers fairs and vocational 'expos' and speak with several people who are working in jobs that interest you. Through these visits, you can ask yourself, 'Are these the types of people I would like to work with on a daily basis? Are they my type of people?' The answers to these questions are based upon your first impressions, but these are important feelings and your visits to the careers fairs and expos are important as well.

In order to get a practical view about the day-to-day work of the people you are visiting, ask the following four questions during your time with them:

1 What are the day-to-day satisfactions in your work?
2 What aspects of your work do you find displeasing?

3 Is this job area expanding with good prospects for future employment?

4 If you could restructure your career, what changes would you make?

Having met some workers, you should have a much more realistic idea about the types of work which prompted your initial interest. Perhaps you have decided to delete one or two possible job areas, but on the other hand, you may now have a much more positive feeling about another. The more positive you can feel about your possible career, the better you are likely to do in your studies. Nothing beats feeling good.

Make an enlarged business card

Enlarging a business card might sound just a bit over the top, but surprisingly, it can really give you a lift. Here's what you can do to experience this positive effect.

Use a word processor (or pen and paper) to make a business card with your name, followed by as many degrees and professional society initials as you wish. On a subsequent line, place the professional title which you aspire to hold. You can add a very prestigious address and note your contact numbers and details (phone, fax, mobile phone, pager and email address). You can also add 'Consultations by appointment only' if that applies to the type of work which you would like to do. Then enlarge the card to poster size on a photocopier. One student even added a totally outrageous hourly fee, which would quickly make him a millionaire.

Look at the sample on page 26, made by a very frustrated second year medical student (name has been changed). The business card was placed on the wall in front of 'Robert's' desk. Every time he looked up from his books, he saw the poster reminding him of his career goal. Instead of mentally wandering off into a prolonged daydream, Robert was prompted to return to his studies. He reported

---

Dr Robert Q. Public

MB, BS, MD, FRACP, OA
Consultant Physician &
Thoracic Medicine Specialist

Suite 11   Professorial Suite 111
111 Macquarie Street   Prince of Wales
Sydney NSW 2000   Hospital
02 1234 5678   02 8765 4321
Mobile: 088 999 777   E-mail: R.Public@XYZ   Pager: 111 222 333

---

that frequently seeing the business card kept him working when fatigue, boredom or other distractions were limiting his concentration. Try it, and see how it can work for you.

Find a study partner(s)—the pacemaker program

If you have ever been involved in serious sport, you probably will have experienced the benefits of training with a partner of comparable, or slightly better, skill and stamina. Most coaches will readily support a program of dual training—that is, you and a partner attack the training exercises and try to encourage each other to greater and more sustained effort. Most athletes are very competitive and will not want to be seen slacking during the training sessions by their peers and coaches. If your training partner decides to push ahead and do a further 500 metres and you are just about at the end of your endurance, there is a very good chance that you will turn and take on that extra 500 as well. Had you been training on your own, fatigue might have terminated your training session.

The same principle applies to studying. While you may not be sitting down with a study partner each night, you can certainly keep in close contact with a friend and exchange study and revision programs once or twice a week. At these meetings, compare notes on how you are going. If your partner is clearly doing more work, then you are more likely to push yourself a bit harder to catch up and maintain the pace.

In addition to pace setting, you might also discuss with your partner sharing study resources. Library books, photocopying duties, class notes and any other resources which you both need, but not all of the time, can be shared. You stand to save time and sometimes money, but most important, you also stand to gain better grades in your assignments from working with your study partner.

Take study breaks

Students take too few study breaks! This might sound like a heavenly statement, but to put it into correct perspective, I'm talking about short, disciplined breaks of say one to two minutes three or four times an hour.

Aside from giving you a rest, will these study breaks increase your motivation? If they are applied regularly, your motivation level should certainly increase. By resting your mind periodically, your concentration on your work will improve, which should benefit you during your exams. Better exam performance will definitely increase your motivation.

If that doesn't sound too complex, try it. Break your study sessions up into shorter periods and take regular breaks. Don't try to phone the current love of your life during these short periods, as you'll only end up frustrating yourself—you won't enjoy the phone conversation that much and you won't get too much done after the break.

Use money as a motivator

Money has been used by some families as a prompter to stimulate more motivation. Using dollars to promote more study activity might be called outright bribery, and of course it really is. However, for many students, money works.

You will need to find a money donor to whom you can report your study progress. Generally, this would be a kind-hearted parent (or a panicky one), but wealthy relatives, family friends, or any other generous soul might do. The supreme task is to convince a suitable person that your increased study activities are worth their investment. You will need to be very convincing, but if this is the only way to get you motivated, then try it. Good luck!

Use self-adhesive notes

Those pads of sticky-backed note sheets make ideal prompters for your study goals. The pads are relatively cheap and you can post the notes at strategic locations— the bathroom mirror, on the door knob of your study place, steering wheel of the car, the telephone, and sundry other locations. These notes with strongly worded messages remind you to get to work on specific tasks. Try them.

Try the 15 x 4 technique

The 15 × 4 technique is probably one of the most effective motivators for students facing full and complicated days. This method will not only motivate you, it will also increase your powers of concentration, the topic discussed in the next chapter. Here's how the 15 × 4 process works.

Use a notebook to keep your daily 'To do' lists. When you are ready to start a study session, note very specifically what you want to get done in the next fifteen minutes. Then note the time when you start the task. When you have completed your first task, place a tick in a column marked 'Done'. Then take a one-minute break before repeating the sequence with a new study task. In summary: note it, do it, tick it, one minute break.

Let's look at a sample page to see how it might be set up.

Tasks	Time	Done
Revise class notes, English	8.00	✓
Plan English essay	8.16	✓
Phone Jack about History Assn.	8.32	✓
Read History, pp. 47–51	8.42	✓
Summary notes, History reading	9.02	✓
Scan History Ch. 3	9.20	✓
Maths problems	9.38	✓
More maths problems	9.55	✓

You will note several features from the above 'To do' list. First, not every task was finished in fifteen minutes. It is difficult to know exactly how long a particular task will take, but you will get better at your estimates with some practice. It is very important to carry on until you have completed your nominated task so you can record your tick in the final column. The phone call to Jack actually took only ten minutes and a one-minute break was not required after this particular activity, so the student carried straight on with the next task. On the last two tasks, the mathematics problems, it is generally difficult to know beforehand how long it will take to solve a particular problem, so it is OK to be a bit more general here and simply note 'maths problems' and then do as much as you can in the fifteen-minute period.

You might ask how this process can motivate you. Look at the log book notations recorded above and you will see on the right-hand side of the page eight ticks, representing study tasks completed. There is nothing like success to make you feel more motivated to carry on to the next task, and then to repeat the process the next day.

ADRIAN—INITIALLY NO MOTIVATION

Adrian was a first year student in mechanical engineering when he sought advice at the Counselling Service about whether to discontinue his course. He had performed very well at high school, mostly because 'the teachers pushed us along with nightly assignments and regular tests'. However, at university, the situation was very different. He alone was responsible for what he did, or didn't do, each evening. Having performed reasonably well in his university entrance exams, he was fairly casual and overly confident about his university studies in his first semester.

His confidence level was shattered when he received his first semester results: failures in three-quarters of his subjects! He knew that he had been 'easing off a bit', but he never expected to *fail*!

Adrian decided that his second semester had to be different, or he was going to be on 'show cause'—asked by the university to show cause why he should be allowed to re-enrol. We discussed his plan—more daily study, regular weekend revision and early preparation for exams. He made daily goals in his diary and ticked off the jobs as he finished them. He also teamed up with Paul, another first year engineering student who had performed quite well in his first semester. The two of them met several times a week to discuss their progress—one of the times being a Thursday lunchtime revision session. I encouraged Adrian to also plan for his leisure hours so that he could enjoy a reasonably balanced life.

By the end of the second semester, the picture was dramatically different. Adrian performed very well throughout the semester and finished in the top half of his class. He was quite convinced that he could perform even better the following year, now that he knew what the university system was like and how to get himself organised for the work load. In essence, he had more confidence in himself and his abilities.

IMPROVING YOUR CONFIDENCE—A MOTIVATION BOOSTER

Just about everyone would like to be more confident, a very critical quality for study and exam success. But how do you become more confident? In a single word, *experience*. That's easily said, but getting the experience to boost your confidence is another matter altogether.

There are three common study areas in which many students report a lack of confidence—taking class notes, writing major essays and, finally, doing exams. Increasing your confidence in each of these three critical areas is basically a matter of practice, but the techniques vary in each case.

Classroom note-taking

Increasing your confidence in classroom note-taking can be accomplished in the comfort of your living room—while watching TV! That might sound absolutely bewildering, but fascinating. Sit down to watch the 30-minute evening news with clipboard, paper and pen. Try to take detailed notes on every news story so that you have a reasonably full account at the end of the program. If you want a check on the clarity of your notes, have a family member or friend read them and then give you a mark out of ten. Carry out this exercise several times a week for a month or so and your note-taking competence and confidence will shoot upwards.

It is important to add that the TV notes you take will probably differ from your classroom experiences. Don't worry—the aim of this exercise is to increase your speed, accuracy and confidence. If you want to consider different styles of notes and techniques, read the 'Notetaking' chapter in *Study Skills for Successful Students* (F. E. Orr, Allen & Unwin, Sydney, 1992).

Essays and assignments

Many students report that they have no confidence in their ability to write essays and assignments. Basically, lack of confidence in essay writing is due to lack of sufficient practice. In order to improve, what should you do? Practise.

One fairly painless way to do this is to make arrangements with an English tutor or someone who is competent in English grammar and syntax. Ask if he or she would be prepared to read two short essays (about 250 words each) a week and make any necessary corrections. You then consider the marker's notations and write another essay for submission. By practising your writing skills and getting lots of feedback, one thing is certainly going to happen—you will improve! The flow-on effect from this improvement will be an increase in your confidence.

Exams

Just as you can increase your confidence in essay writing with mini-essays and lots of feedback, the same applies to exams. Either you can set mini-exams or you can join a student syndicate in which each student submits questions for a group exam. Working through a number of these syndicate exams (conducted under exam time conditions) will help you with your revision, time management skills and even apparently trivial matters (except for the marker), such as handwriting legibility. The more practice exams you can do, the better you will perform when those major exams come along.

SUMMARY

Keeping motivated is very important, especially for passing exams. Plan your study activities in your diary, use the 15 × 4 technique and find a friend with whom you can pace yourself. Practising your note-taking, essay writing and examination skills will also boost your motivation.

3

Concentrate better

'Depend upon it, Sir, when a man knows he is to be hanged in a fortnight, it concentrates his mind wonderfully.' — Samuel Johnson, 1777

Concentration is a skill, much like bike riding, ice skating, roller blading and car driving. Most people can develop more powerful concentration, but considerable training and practice are required. You will need some instruction on how to do it and then plenty of practice trying it before you can reliably say that 'my concentration power is strong, dependable and productive!'

Before launching into the training, complete the following checklist to see if you have any trouble spots, as well as strong points (no sense training where there is considerable competency—your valuable time is better spent on other parts of this book!).

Concentration checklist

☐ I often feel tired when I sit down to study.

☐ There is too much noise around my study area.
☐ I usually study with the radio tuned to my favourite music station.
☐ I am not interested in many of the subjects I am meant to be studying.
☐ I do not feel confident about the subjects I'm enrolled in.
☐ I generally feel depressed when I have to study.
☐ I do not know what I want to do when I finish my course.
☐ I miss watching TV when hunched over my desk.
☐ There are too many conflicts in my life at present.
☐ I would rather be out having fun than studying.

How many ticks did you record? If you scored more than five, then it might be a very good idea to sit down with a counsellor who is experienced in educational and study matters and review your situation. As I said above, concentration is a complex mental process and you will need to clear as many obstacles from both your mind and your immediate environment in order to function well. If you scored three or less on the checklist, you could skim this chapter and then go on to more critical matters in this book.

Before jumping right into the basics, let's look at the case of David, who came to me with some significant concentration problems.

DAVID—POTENTIALLY BRIGHT, BUT FREQUENTLY FOGGED

David was tested for academic aptitude in year 10 and the results showed that he had outstanding potential to excel at school and certainly later at university. However, he performed far less brilliantly in years 11 and 12, but did scrape into a good university.

During his final two years at high school, his parents noticed that he often appeared vague and 'elsewhere'. His teachers commented that he did not mentally attend to the discussions in class and he often seemed totally lost. The crunch came when David was playing football and, in an important game, ran the wrong way with the ball, scoring a goal for the opposition. His coaches were initially irate, but then totally bewildered. His teachers were not surprised. In subsequent discussions, they were all in agreement that David needed professional assistance. He was referred to me to help him concentrate more fully—regardless of what he was doing.

David reported that in class, and occasionally on the playing field, he just 'wandered off' mentally. He was quite creative and artistic and he said, 'my mind just becomes easily distracted by fleeting thoughts and impulses'. As he was accustomed to training exercises for football and other sports, I thought it might be best to start with the familiar and work onwards from there. In conjunction with his coaches, David kept track of any concentration lapses when out on the practice field or in strategy discussions in the coaches' briefing room. His coaches also observed him carefully to see if he was following the set activities.

At the end of a week of record keeping, David was quite surprised how frequently he lost concentration. Rather than penalise David for these lapses, his coaches tried to find times when he did focus on the matter at hand and then they complimented him appropriately. David slowly improved—it would be nice to say that he *immediately* improved, but that simply was not the case.

In the classroom, one of the most practical exercises which helped David keep track of discussions was self-directed questions. I told David to frequently ask himself, 'Where is the teacher going with this topic? How is it related to the issue discussed just before?'. These questions were aimed at helping David to maintain his concentration and keep the present topics of discussion clearly in mind. He was also asked to keep quite detailed notes so that he was monitoring the issues both mentally and mechanically. These approaches seemed to work very well.

David finished his university degree with a very respectable pass in engineering. He well knew that fading out while trying to solve a complicated engineering problem was only going to lead to failure.

BASIC TRAINING FOR CONCENTRATION IMPROVEMENT

There are three major situations where educational concentration is really critical: in the classroom, at home doing homework, and during exams. You can improve your concentration in each of these situations by practising the following exercises.

In the classroom

Many students find that they frequently lose concentration during classroom discussions. The loss of concentration might be due to many causes, such as fatigue, boredom or lack of interest, to name but a few. It is important to realise that many experiences in life are not going to be fascinating and entertaining. There will be more than a fair amount of fairly basic and perhaps even boring study issues which must be attended to, and even concentrated upon. So, how can you beat boredom?

Mental warm-ups

Just as serious athletes warm-up their muscles before getting actively involved in a game or even practice, students should do the same. Think of your mind as a mental muscle. You need to stretch it and get it moving with some gentle exercises before throwing it into high level activity—and full concentration certainly is a high level mental activity. The mental warm-ups are quite easy—they take only about five minutes before you start your class or homework session. One recommended exercise is skimming over your class notes: note the major concepts and issues; pay particular attention to any diagrams or charts; and be sure you have a general idea of what was covered. Another warm-up activity to use before a class is to skim the relevant chapter in your text. Note the major themes—focus upon the section headings and the items presented in bold face type. By carrying out these warm-ups, you are briefing your mind about what is going to happen in the next class. Having carried out these warm-ups, you can then walk into class ready for action. You will be more confident in your note-taking and more alert and retentive during class discussion.

Self-directed questions

Once you are in the class and listening and note-taking, it is still possible to lose the sharp edge of concentration. If this happens, then try another strategy—ask yourself questions. Self-interrogation is not the aim here. The questions are meant to connect you with what is happening with the teacher. 'What does that term mean? How is it associated with the topics just discussed? Where is the teacher going with this concept?' Questions such as these will help to stimulate your interest and preserve your concentration.

Short breaks

Intense concentration is hard work, so whether you are in class or at home, it is a good practice to take frequent breaks so that you can keep your mind rested. Concentrating fully upon your studies is quite different to performing physical work. You are not likely to produce beads of sweat on your forehead or experience muscular pains. However, you will know when you are getting tired and, at that point, stop for a short break. Stand up, take a few deep breaths, stretch your arms and legs and then sit down and get back to work. These brief breaks will help you to recharge and keep more focused.

Doing homework

Serious students will spend at least several hours studying at home on week-days and perhaps a longer session or two on the weekends doing the major essays, assignments and revising for exams. There are two strategies for boosting your concentration at home.

SQ3R reading technique

Reading is going to account for many hours of your academic work and lapses in concentration will prove to be very wasteful. The SQ3R technique is a structured approach to reading which will assist you to maintain a high level of concentration.

SQ3R is an acronym which stands for *Survey, Question, Read, Recite, Review*. Let's look at each of these processes.

Survey This term means what it says—you survey the entire chapter or section prior to commencing your detailed reading. Just page through the section and note the section headings and subheadings, the diagrams and charts, the bold face and italic print. These are the parts of the chapter which the editors have highlighted and want you to note. They are also a good guide to what the reading will be about.

Question As you survey the section, ask yourself questions about the content. What does a certain term mean? How is it related to the concepts just studied in the previous chapter? These questions will help you to generate some interest in the material to be read and will also establish some mental goals for your reading. You read to answer your questions.

Read This means you start at the beginning and proceed to read the section, paragraph by paragraph, unless you are very rushed and have to skim read. As you read, try to answer the questions previously posed about the major terms you come across. Your mind should be activated by the former two stages, survey and question, which should help your concentration.

Recite After you finish reading perhaps three or four paragraphs, pause briefly and recite the major points covered. Continue to pause and recite frequently so that you can be certain that you have been concentrating and retaining the major points.

Review Having read the chapter or section, go over the major points before finishing your study session. You may wish to review the points again within the next 24 hours, as repetition is a great teacher.

Revision for exams

When preparing for exams, an associated technique may be helpful: read, write, revise. Read through your notes or textbook sections, and then write just very brief notes focusing upon major terms and concepts. Do *not* write extensive notes, as writing is very time expensive. The purpose of the writing exercise is to apply your learning in a practical way and to utilise a different part of your brain. You can then use these brief notes as a revision resource in future study sessions.

In exams

Maintaining concentration during exams is critical, as any lapses here will cost you valuable marks. Always take several different coloured pens to every exam. When you read the questions, especially complicated essay questions, underline with a blue or black pen the topics and terms which are central to the question. Then re-read the question and this time underline the operational terms—that is, terms which instruct you to carry out certain processes, such as 'critically discuss', 'compare and contrast' and 'trace the development of'. Having read the questions twice and underlined these terms, it is more likely that you will have focused upon the central issues to be addressed.

Practical pointers for increased concentration

- Start study sessions with small, warm-up tasks and work towards more complex ones.
- Always work to pre-set goals.
- Take *brief* notes to apply your knowledge.
- When losing concentration, take a short break: stand, stretch, take three breaths and get back to work.

- For really weak concentration levels, practise listening and note-taking with the 30-minute evening news broadcast.
- In class, always try to sit in the front—distractions are then behind you.
- When reading or listening in class, ask yourself topical questions.
- Listen for good exam questions during discussions by your teacher.
- Study your most difficult subject in a student syndicate—learn from your classmates.
- At home, wear a T-shirt or some other 'uniform' when you sit down to study.
- Eliminate as many distractions as possible when you are studying.
- In exams, take frequent but short breaks.
- Reward yourself when you have completed a study task while concentrating well.

SUMMARY

Concentrating effectively is hard work, but doing mental warm-up exercises before your classes and your evening study sessions will improve your efficiency. Use the SQ3R technique to boost your concentration while reading. Underlining or highlighting will also help you to focus on the important terms.

4

Manage your time

'I've got plenty of time! My exams don't start for another two days.'
— Student who later failed

Time is an important convention. We all depend upon it. In fact, we need to know that timetables and schedules work so we won't be late. However, keeping to time, not wasting time, and saving time are three challenges which most students would like to conquer. In order to see how you rate on these timely topics, complete the following checklist.

Time management checklist

☐ I am frequently late for classes.
☐ I often submit my work late.
☐ My studying gets done in a helter-skelter fashion.
☐ I waste a lot of time being indecisive.
☐ Friends frequently interrupt my studies and waste my time.

☐ My teachers get tired of me asking for extensions on major assignments.

☐ I have difficulty walking away from a good TV show.

☐ I procrastinate about starting major projects.

☐ I waste time re-arranging the papers on my desk before starting to study.

☐ I find completing tasks to be difficult—I want them to be perfect.

How did you score? Most of us would certainly have ticked several of the items, as efficient time management is a challenge for most people. However, if you ticked five or more items, then you need to look very carefully at your time management skills. The importance of managing your time very well may be seen in the following case study of Martina, a first year university English major.

MARTINA—ALWAYS LATE

Martina was the eldest of three children and the first person in her family to attend a university. While her parents did not overtly push her to succeed, Martina did find that there were frequent arguments at home about the lateness of her homework, school projects and exam preparation. 'My parents never stop hassling me about my school work,' Martina frequently complained.

In her early high school years, Martina was very diligent and tried to complete all her homework before dinner. However, in the later years, she started watching some of the popular soap operas on TV and fell behind in her homework. As Martina was very bright, she was able to get away with more TV and less homework until year 12. The pressures from her parents, and particularly from her school teachers, finally convinced her that studying in front of the TV was really a waste of time and that it was necessary to get serious about her work. She retreated to her room and applied herself to her reading, revision, essays and exams.

Martina started carrying revision cards to study on the bus and train. While walking her dog, she listened to tapes of the plays and books she was studying so she could fully understand the characters and plots. Probably the most helpful time saver was limiting her telephone calls to one 20-minute period per evening.

Having mastered these time management skills in year 12, Martina felt overly confident and thought she could coast along comfortably at university. It took only a few weeks for her to realise that her university studies were in fact much more complex and demanding than her high school work. She was wise enough to consult the Counselling Service for help before she became too lost in the ever growing pile of work.

From the discussions with her counsellor, Martina found that many of her time-saving techniques from year 12 were applicable to her university studies. But Martina also wanted to get to know many of her fellow students, and these meetings often meant hours of time in the coffee lounge or university bar. She decided that she would have to become more disciplined about how she spent her free time. Martina organised lunches with friends, but kept the free hours in the morning and afternoon for study in the library.

By applying more discipline, Martina was able to finish her first year with a distinction average. Had she not applied a more rigorous approach to her schedule and studies, her first year results might well have been far less impressive.

MINIMISE WASTED TIME

How much time do you think you waste each day? I asked 200 students that question and most were not able to come up with an accurate answer. Rather than guess, I asked them to participate in a study of their wasted time. They kept a two-week log of the times and places where they felt they had wasted time. What do you think the average amount of wasted time per day was? Sixty-four minutes a day—not a colossal figure, but when multiplied over a week, a month and a year, you obtain some fairly large figures:

Average wasted time

1 week	7.5 hours
1 month	32 hours
1 year	384 hours

For most students, that final figure, 384 wasted hours per year, really hurts, especially if that time could be productively used in the final weeks of the semester or year. The best way to approach the wasted time problem is to prevent it. Try each day to use your time as efficiently as possible. One step towards that goal is to be aware of how and where you are wasting time.

Log of wasted time

Estimating your time wasting can be very simple. Just carry a pocket notebook and note the following factors every time you become aware that you are wasting time:

Wasted time log

When: _____

Where: _____

With whom: _____

Why? _____

Total time wasted: _____

Most of the items on this log sheet are straightforward, except perhaps the 'Why?' item. You may have to dig deeply into the history of your entrenched habits to answer

this question. For example, why were you unable to say to Helen, 'No, I can't talk now; I have my essay to finish' or 'Tom, let's talk about this project tomorrow when we both have had time to prepare'?

Many of your time wasters might touch on sensitive personal issues, such as failure to assert yourself in front of others or failure to exercise sufficient personal discipline. These are very important self-management skills and need to be sharpened if you think they are a bit dull. If so, see a counsellor and discuss how you can make some improvements and save lots of time.

SOURCES OF WASTED TIME

Given that time is the arch enemy of most students—too much to do and not enough time to do it!—you are well advised to reduce wasted time as much as possible. 'But where should I start?' many of you might ask. Studies of time use and mis-use among university students show several major areas where time has been frequently wasted and therefore might be saved.

Television

Many of you might claim that if you don't get your 'hit' of at least two or more hours of TV per day, you will go into withdrawal. While TV might seem to be an essential part of life, it really is not. In fact, if you want to be very serious about limiting this area of time wastage, get rid of your TV set. However, if you live with others, that will not make you the most popular person in the house. Instead of resorting to this fairly severe solution, are there any other ways of controlling your TV watching?

- Be a selective TV viewer. Schedule the one or two shows you want to watch each day, but make watching contingent upon achieving some of your study goals.
- Stand up while watching. That might sound strange, but it takes much more energy to get up than to sit down in a comfortable lounge chair. TV watching can become too comfortable and getting out of that chair can be a major chore. If you stay standing, however, you avoid the problem.
- Do two things at once. TV watching does not usually require full concentration. Do some stretching or other form of exercise, browse through some magazines, sew, file, write to friends, or even talk on the telephone.
- Set the oven timer. If you are weak (and most of us are), set the timer to go off at the end of the show. When you hear the 'BZZZZZZ', it's time to turn the set off and get back to your books.
- Move the TV to an inconvenient location. Watch TV shows in the dampness of your garage where oil fumes

and the occasional mouse might interrupt your enjoyment. Other family members might object, but you will also spend less time watching the box.

- Use a video recorder to tape your preferred shows—then watch them at a more convenient time.

The TV set can pose a major time problem, but be prepared, be strong and be persistent. The battle can be won and you will achieve better academic results by studying more and watching less.

Telephone

Just as some students might think they need two to three hours of exposure to TV a day to continue living, others hold a similar view about telephone talk time. Contrary to these beliefs, it *is* possible to get through 24 hours without speaking on the telephone, unless there is a life-endangering situation to cope with.

The telephone situation has become more complex lately with the advent of mobile phones. Many students now carry them and, certainly, they are a convenience, but definitely not a necessity. If you have a mobile phone, be careful not to overuse it, as (1) it's expensive; and (2) unnecessary talk time robs you of valuable study time. Here are some pointers on how to control your telephone talking.

- Schedule a telephone period each evening. Rather than be interrupted during a particularly productive study session, plan a 20-minute period when you make all your calls.
- Plan the time duration for each call. Tell the other party how much time you have available and work to that deadline. 'I've got to go now' is a perfectly acceptable concluding statement for a busy student.

- Use an egg timer or the oven timer to remind you when your telephone period is exhausted (even if you are not out of wind).
- Ask frequent callers to call at a convenient time.
- Use an answering machine to record messages while you are studying or have messages taken by a house-mate.
- Consult your local telephone sales office for information about telephones with tone off or do not disturb functions.
- If you are really audacious, hang up on the other party, but only when you are in mid-sentence. They will blame the phone system, as no one could be so self-effacing as to hang up on oneself.

Waiting time

- Carry study materials (palm-sized flash cards, notes, books) with you and study during those small amounts of waiting time.
- Avoid those long waits at doctors and dentists by calling ahead to see if they are on schedule.
- Make audiotapes of notes and replay them while waiting, walking, washing up or doing other mechanical tasks.
- Have your study materials adapted for windy or wet conditions—plastic binders for notes, plastic bag for note cards.

Commuting time

Many students who do not live on campus spend up to four or possibly more hours per day commuting to campus. Try to arrange your travel time so that you can spend at least two-thirds of this time studying. It will take some effort to concentrate while commuting, but with practice, you can revise notes, tapes or cards almost anywhere—even standing up on buses and trains (use flash cards here).

- Buses and trains can be used for some study. Plan ahead for the situation and have flash cards, tapes and notes available for in transit revision.
- When driving, use tapes for revision. Learn an idea at every red traffic light.
- When walking, revise a concept every time you wait at the kerbside for the traffic light to change.
- If you travel with classmates, have a brief discussion about the class topics presented that day.

Uninvited visitors

- Keep your door closed and perhaps even locked when you are studying.
- Place a 'Do not disturb' sign on your door.
- Do not have a chair at your deskside. Visitors have great difficulty getting up and out of that chair within twenty minutes of sitting down.
- If a visitor comes into your room, do not allow them to sit down. Tell them that you are busy and arrange another time to visit.
- If you live in a student resident hall and you hear the hall gossip walking towards your room, jump out of your seat and meet the person in the hallway. You have more control over your time when on your feet, as standing conversations take less time.
- For very thick-hided visitors, simply tell them you cannot talk now and usher them away from your work place. If you are feeling guilty about turning the individual away, make an arrangement to see the person at a more convenient time.

SAYING NO!

From the preceding section, you will know that being appropriately assertive is very important in saving your study time. Many people get worried about saying 'no' to others because they feel they will not be liked or respected.

The opposite is often the case. People respect others who can appropriately protect their time.

From a more personal viewpoint, if you walk away from encounters having said 'yes', when you really wanted to say 'no', it is very likely that you will be feeling angry at yourself. Life is just too short to go around feeling continually angry, so it is far better to do something constructive about the problem.

You can become more comfortable saying 'no' by simply practising in the privacy of your bathroom. Look into the mirror and imagine the target person to whom you want to say 'no'. Practise that short but important word over and over with different amounts of volume and types of inflection until you have mastered the skill. It might sound silly and you might feel slightly embarrassed in your bathroom, but it works.

ELECTRONIC MARVELS

Before leaving this chapter on time management, attention must be given to the electronic marvels which make the work of the student much more manageable: personal computers (PCs), facsimile machines, electronic mail (email) and the Internet.

Personal computers

PCs have revolutionised the work life of students. They can be used to process essays, compute statistics, maintain diaries, and do a wide range of other tasks which previously took vast amounts of time. Today, every student should take the opportunity of knowing at least how to operate a PC and use some of the basic software, specifically word processing. Almost every employer who will be reviewing your resume will want to know that you have these basic skills.

Laptop computers have made studying on campus, at home or any other place perfectly possible. As already suggested, the studying activities can include essay writing, note filing, problem solving and many other types of student activities. Laptop computers are still quite expensive for many student budgets, but the prices seem to be going down and down. If you are thinking about buying a computer, consider buying a laptop so you have the advantage of taking your computer with you. One word of warning though: laptop computers can be easily stolen, so be very careful about security. As a precaution, you could have your name and driver's licence number engraved onto a visible part of the computer as a deterrent against theft—or at least as an aid to police should your computer be stolen.

Facsimile machines

The 'fax' machine has proved to be a major asset to students who are either studying via distance education or who are generally late in meeting their submission deadlines. While not many students will have a fax machine at home, they will almost certainly have access to one somewhere nearby. If you do not know a friend with a fax machine, most post offices or newsagents will send your message for a small fee.

If you are running late with your assignment, there are several distinct advantages in submitting it via fax (with the approval of your teacher) as opposed to shoving it under your teacher's door. Probably the most important advantage is that the date and time of sending will be recorded on the paper. The second major advantage is that your paper will be printed out in the school office as opposed to being shoved under the door or stuffed into the input box. Many student papers have gone missing after being placed in such boxes. The third advantage is that you save time and energy, especially if you live a long distance from the school office. If you do submit an essay by fax, send a paper copy as well because fax ink does not last and fax paper is generally of lower quality.

Email and the Internet

Electronic mail, or email for short, and the Internet have probably been two of the most positive prompters of correspondence since the invention of the ballpoint pen. Messages whizz along the cables (some delays can occur) and can link people from across the world without using stationery or stamps. Once you have a computer, a modem and a connection to an email provider, all you need is the email address of the recipient.

Email can provide easy access to anyone anywhere in the world for most universities and their staff. You can contact your teaching staff to follow up on lecture points and discuss research problems or any other academic concerns. Most university staff are very proficient at using email and would see email as being an efficient and effective way of keeping in touch with their students. If you haven't tapped into the email system yet, get started and discover how it can change your academic life.

The Internet can help you to collect information without stepping outside your home. You can carry out library searches and obtain information from a vast array of different sources 'on the net', but be careful about being drawn into spending too much time wandering about the Internet system, or 'surfing the net' as the experts say.

SUMMARY

Time is your arch enemy, especially when you have numerous assignments to prepare plus revision for exams. Try to eliminate wasted time by studying 'on the run'—use flashcards, listen to tapes, and control time in front of the TV and on the phone. Use a PC and the email and Internet systems to make your studying efficient.

5

Improve your memory

'I was very well prepared for the exam, but somehow I had forgotten the correct day. I turned up at the right time, but one day late, and now they want to fail me!' — Student with a major memory problem

Memory is the life blood of most students. The wisest words presented in classrooms, the sagest phrases written in books, and the most studious advice given by teaching staff are all next to worthless if they cannot be remembered. Yes, we would all like to have better memories, but the regrettable truth is that hard work, often very hard work, is involved.

Paul, a close friend with a double first class honours degree from Cambridge University, has a marvellous memory. He recently was invited to be a member of our trivial pursuit team at a community function. After leading our team to a most decisive and repeated victory (we won last year to the chagrin of other contestants!), someone on a neighbouring table asked him, 'How can you possibly

remember all of those really trivial facts?'. Paul, after some careful thought, said, 'I have great difficulty forgetting things'. Wouldn't it be nice if we all had Paul's difficulty?

To be fair to Paul, he spends a large amount of time reading, studying, writing, consulting and, alas, remembering many things. Even if you have the most energetic and retentive mind, such as Paul's, good memory means hard work. For the mere mortals of this world who have only average minds, good memory means practice, practice and more practice.

Let's look at what you can do to improve your memory. Perhaps the first thing to ask is, 'Just how good, bad or indifferent is my memory?'. Complete the following check-list to see where you might be experiencing difficulties.

Memory checklist

☐ I frequently cannot recall what I have just read in the last two pages.

☐ If it were not for my lecture notes, I would have little recall of the lecture contents.

☐ Daydreaming is a frequent problem for me, especially in 'boring' classes.

☐ When beginning my exam revision, I often feel discouraged at how little I can retain.

☐ I am often embarrassed by not being able to recall the names of people I have met in classes.

☐ Even though I summarise my reading assignments, I find it difficult to remember the major points.

☐ I generally go through my notes three times before exams, but some concepts still seem fuzzy.

☐ Studying 'boring' subjects impedes my memory.

☐ Pre-exam anxiety wrecks my memory.

☐ I tend to read through my books too quickly, with little time for recall.

Most of you will have ticked several of these memory items. If you scored more than six or seven in the checklist, then you certainly need to tackle this chapter—and actively apply some of the techniques so that your memory can improve. If you scored three or less, maybe your time is better spent pushing on to another chapter which might have more immediate relevance—your memory powers are probably in good order.

LARRY AND MERCINDA—FRUSTRATIONS OF INDIVIDUAL DIFFERENCES

Larry and Mercinda were medical students, who both had good memories, but there were some interesting differences between the two students.

Larry was very bright and capable. He seemed to be able to attend lectures, at least most of them, and do very little more than rush through his notes lightly before the exams and pass quite easily. Mercinda, on the other hand, attended every lecture, took impeccable notes, studied her textbooks and notes several times and then, with considerable difficulty, just passed her exams. During one of their many exam 'post mortems', Mercinda seemed particularly frustrated. She asked Larry, who was appearing very casual about the exam and his performance, what he did to retain the information. Larry said that he listened to his lectures and often juggled the information in his mind. Sometimes, he created rhymes, ditties and songs (he was very musical). At other times he constructed mind maps, making constellations or other graphic figures with the information patterns.

Mercinda was fascinated by Larry's response. She had never considered making rhymes, songs or mind maps of her biochemistry formulae or physiology notes. Having discovered the 'secret' to Larry's success, she tried to put the theory into practice. Her early attempts just produced more frustration, as she felt she was just not sufficiently creative. Larry agreed to help Mercinda develop some creative tools for processing her notes. He asked her to look at a concept which she wanted to remember and to look for rhyming words, graphic potentials, or simply for some contortion, such as turning it upside down or inside out. Once again, this was new territory for Mercinda, but she agreed to try these techniques over the next month.

During that month, Mercinda and Larry met for coffee and swapped notes on their creative efforts. As you would expect, Larry produced some astonishing creations while

Mercinda struggled with just a few. However, Mercinda enjoyed the challenge and over the succeeding months she became better and better at it. All of this creative practice (for example, singing tunes in the shower about the Krebs Cycle in biochemistry) was also helping her to remember her notes.

Both Larry and Mercinda finished their medical degrees with Larry really preferring to be a concert pianist. Mercinda became a very successful general practitioner who also taught beginning medical students some memory techniques for passing exams.

MEMORY METHODS

As suggested above, there are several methods which you can use to improve your memory. Above all, the essence is to *use* the information you want to remember. It doesn't really matter too much whether you read it, recite it, sing it or dance it (those last two options might strain your creative talents somewhat), you are helping the memory process every time the information is *used*.

Every time you pass any thought through the nerve pathways of your brain, you will find it easier to retrieve that information. Essentially, this is what revision is all about—retracing specific pathways among the millions of neurons in your brain. Much like creating a new pathway across an unmarked grassy field—the more you use the same pathway, the easier it becomes to retrace your steps.

Creative associations

You will be better able to remember facts, figures, concepts and theories if they can be associated with some interesting image. Let's look at an example.

I attended a memory workshop some years ago and the leader greeted each of the 50 or so participants at the doorway. He introduced himself and then engaged each participant in a brief conversation before greeting the next person. Halfway through the workshop, he said he would try to demonstrate how his memory techniques worked. He said he would try to recall the name of each participant and perhaps some other information which was discussed during the brief doorway conversation. He went from one participant to the next and missed only three names!

I was very impressed, as were the other participants. The workshop leader quickly explained that he carries out this exercise most weekdays, so is very well practised. But how did he do it, above and beyond mere practice? He explained that, on greeting every participant, he used their name at least three or four times: 'Pleased to meet you, Harry. Tell me, Harry, where do you come from? . . . What do you hope to gain from the workshop, Harry? . . . I hope you enjoy the workshop, Harry, and find it helpful in your job'.

Aside from repeating Harry's name, the workshop leader explained that he also looked for some unusual or pronounced quality in Harry's appearance or behaviour. Let's say that Harry had large ears. As he was talking with Harry, the workshop leader might imagine Harry as a large elephant, flapping his ears in flights over the tallest buildings in the city, swooping and soaring with the birds. That image would make Harry very memorable and help the leader to retrieve Harry's name.

Generally, the more outrageous the imagery, the more memorable will be the associated item. This technique requires some practice in creative image making. If you practise every time you meet someone new, you will quickly find that your memory for names has improved.

Mnemonics

The spelling for this word, mnemonics, might pose a memory problem, unless of course you are a student of the Greek language—it comes from a Greek word, *mnemonikos*, meaning, you guessed it, 'of memory'. I initially used mnemonics when I was a first year medical student and had to memorise almost entire books, one of which included the twelve cranial nerves. We used a mnemonic: 'On Old Olympus's Towering Top, A Fair Armed Golfer Viewed Some Hops'. The first letter of each word was the first letter of each of the twelve cranial nerves. Generally, all of us remembered the mnemonic very well, but some students said they could not retrieve the names of the nerves (they were the ones who didn't make it into year II). If you are going to use mnemonics, be very certain that you can utilise both phases of the exercise, as quoting only the rhyme to an examiner is not going to win you any marks!

Remembering what you read

In chapter 3 we discussed the SQ3R technique as a means of increasing your concentration. It will also increase your memory for the material being read.

You will recall that the acronym SQ3R stands for: Survey, Question, Read, Recite, Review. Each of the five steps involves some use of the information being read. By carrying out the process, you have increased your memory potential by applying the concepts in five different ways: initially as a survey; then by asking yourself questions about the major headings; then by reading section by section; followed by a brief recitation of the major points; and finally, by reviewing the entire reading task. Your retention will certainly be increased by using the SQ3R.

Remembering in class

Just as you can increase your memory during reading by using the information in different ways, you can also increase your memory for what is said in classes by using a slightly different, but similar technique, called WLQNR— Warm-up, Listen, Question, Note, Revise.

Warming up for your classes starts before you enter the classroom. Either the night before or during the day of your classes, spend about three to five minutes per subject browsing through the relevant chapter of the reference text, noting section headings, bold face and italic print, charts, graphs and other visual aids. Your mission is not to learn all the terms and topics at this stage, just to become familiar with them.

The listening part is fairly straightforward. You listen actively during the class, trying to follow the line of argument. Be sure to focus on the major points of the presentation. Your warm-up prior to class should help here.

The questioning function is just what it says—you ask yourself questions about the topics and issues as they are being presented. For example, 'What connection does the *light reaction* have to the *dark reaction* during *photosynthesis?*'. Asking yourself questions will stimulate your attention and also enhance your memory.

Noting the major points is very important as you are generating your prime revision source for later study. Don't try to note everything said in class, as much will be irrelevant. Just get the major points. You can add to your notes later.

Revision of the major topics from your class lectures should be done as soon as possible after the conclusion of your classes. If possible, remain seated at the end of class or go to the library and scan the headings of your notes. This revision will help to reinforce the associations of the points and will also improve your memory.

Memory, revision and exams

Most students hate revision and I can well understand why—revision generally precedes examinations which are often associated with high anxiety. The anxiety spreads from the exams to the revision.

How can you conquer the revision tasks? You should quickly respond, 'Start early!'. That's absolutely critical, because learning well takes time—and those panicky hours the night before your assessment will not be sufficient for most students.

While revising, take frequent but short study breaks so that your mind gets some rest and relief. Revision is hard work and your brain will suffer from fatigue. If you don't rest occasionally, your efficiency will drop sharply after several hours.

The revision process is best conducted as multiple readings and applications (recite, write brief notes, write exam questions and then answer them) of the topics. Initially, read through your notes and focus upon the major headings and important concepts. The first reading should be fairly rapid. Don't expect to be able to recall very much—you will only frustrate yourself if you do. Then read through your notes again, keeping the pace up so that you have time for multiple revisions. Once again, don't expect retention miracles even after the second revision. Things should begin to look a bit brighter after the third and fourth revisions, as familiarity turns to certainty—you will begin to know that you know the topics! By the fifth or sixth time, you should begin smiling to yourself as you work through your notes and almost see the next page before the page is turned. Ideally, that is the level of knowledge you should have before you enter the exam room.

SUMMARY

Memory is probably your most important mental function during your student years. Warm up your brain before each class, use creative imagery when taking notes and revise these notes *many* times before your exams. Ideally, you want to know that you know your notes when you walk into the exam room.

Tool Box

- Use coloured pens, highlighters, self-adhesive note sheets to make your notes colourful and therefore more memorable.

- Convert any suitable concepts to geometric designs—circles, squares, pyramids or other graphic styles. Remember, pictures are worth a thousand words.

- Use acronyms to make learning easier. SCUBA is an acronym for what? Self-Contained Underwater Breathing Apparatus. The acronym is easier to remember.

- Use a diary and schedule weekly revision sessions. Learn your notes routinely on weekends. Don't let them accumulate.

- Use the concepts you are learning—to question, answer, argue, debate, rhyme, sing or dance. Apply the concepts in any other way you can imagine. Remember, information used is information retained.

- Use your senses—smell, touch, sight, sound, or even taste. For example, I learned a lot of my gross anatomy in medical school by feeling my bones and muscles. Using your sense of smell might be difficult unless you are studying to be a chef.

- Use flash cards. Make revision flash cards by writing the topic on one side of a palm-sized index card and any important related information on the reverse side. Secure these cards with a rubber band and carry with you throughout the day, pulling them out and reading through several whenever you have a spare moment.

- Tape-record topic headings followed by a pause and replay tapes while walking, driving, washing up. You fill in the pauses with any relevant details, but keep the tapes rolling whenever possible.

PART II

Performing in your exams

6

Controlling exam nerves

Uncertainty → anxiety
*Certainty about thorough exam preparation → confidence and
calmness*

Every student would like to walk into the exams absolutely confident about the material to be tested. However, this is a very infrequent occurrence. Too often, the preparation is left until too late, sometimes just the night before, and this creates a breeding ground for exam nerves. Walking into the exam room might feel akin to walking into an execution chamber—not a nice feeling at all. Instead of experiencing those negative feelings, you can learn how to replace them with calmness and confidence.

This chapter discusses relaxation training—how you can deal with your nerves well before your exam days. It is very important to start early with your training (it will require two practice sessions each day for about three months) so that you have plenty of time in which to master the skills. The practice exercises are pleasant and

productive and, once you get the hang of it, you will be looking forward to your relaxation sessions each day.

LEARN HOW TO RELAX

Learning how to relax is really the process of conquering worry and other negative thoughts. Most students face exams with very active minds. Unfortunately, the activity might not be all that helpful, as many thoughts might be focused upon improbable questions, difficult markers and many other negative possibilities, including failure.

You might compare the human mind to a team of stagecoach horses racing out of control while the driver is paralysed with fear. In order to gain control, the driver has to work hard at tugging and pulling in the reins to reduce the speed and to redirect the team.

The same condition exists for most people entering a training course in relaxation. Because our minds have been subjected to years and years of stimulation, arousal and provocation, with no time being spent on learning how to quiet the mind, it will be hard but enjoyable work acquiring the skills of relaxation. It is important to emphasise that learning how to relax is a long-term project—that is, about three months of practice will be required to achieve the full effect. Don't be put off by the word 'practice' because it is a most pleasant and enjoyable experience.

The following steps will be a helpful guide to learning the skill.

PRACTISE EVERY DAY

Place 'relaxation practice' on your daily plan and give it a high priority rating. The more you practise, the better you will be able to relax. Even though learning how to relax might sound simple, it's not. You'll have to work at it regularly to perfect the skill.

How much should you practise each day? At the start of your training, several short sessions (three to five minutes) will be helpful. At this stage, longer sessions are likely to give you practice in worrying or daydreaming. As you progressively become more skilled in controlling the activity of your mind, increase the length of the sessions. Ultimately, try to practise for about twenty minutes each day, preferably in two ten-minute sessions.

One word of warning: on very busy days, you may be tempted to put off your practice session altogether. These are the days when it is most important to relax. So, stick to your routine and turn your mind off the pressures of the day and on to the relaxation technique. In addition to giving you valuable practice and a well-needed rest, the time spent relaxing is also forming a firm habit of personal discipline—being able to get to and through the important tasks of each day.

EXPECT TO RELAX

It is important that you develop a positive expectation that you will relax. There is little use in shouting to yourself, 'RELAX, dammit, RELAX!!'. You might try instead saying calmly and decisively: 'I am going to relax now'. Trying too hard will only complicate the process. Just sit back and let it happen.

FIND A QUIET SPOT

You can relax just about anywhere, assuming you can remain undisturbed for a few minutes. If you are at home, take the phone off the hook. If others might call in on you, place a 'Do not disturb' sign on your door. Better yet, tell them you are practising your relaxation skills before you start. If quiet spots are difficult to find during your days, you can still get on with the job.

Many people have found practising on commuter buses and trains perfectly satisfactory. Others practise in their (parked) cars or sitting in a sunny or shady spot in a park or on campus. The important point is to make certain that you fit the practice into your daily schedule. Try to practise in different places and at different times so that the process generalises to a wide variety of situations.

MAKE YOURSELF COMFORTABLE

As implied in the previous step, you really don't need special conditions in which to practise relaxation. Find somewhere comfortable and get started. It is not advisable to stretch out on your bed, especially if you are practising late in the day. There is too much conditioning for your mind to cope with a tired mind and body and the prone position in bed. Before you get to step three or four, you will be sound asleep. So, try to arrange your practice sessions sitting up, or even standing up! One student became quite proficient at practising his relaxation while standing in a crowded commuter train. No one bothered him as he stood there, eyes closed, briefcase between his knees and extended hand gripping the nearby pole. If you choose to practise under these conditions, try to position yourself at the rear of the carriage and certainly not in front of a doorway.

FOCUS ON YOUR BREATHING

To start, close your eyes and focus your attention upon your breathing. Listen to the soft whistling sound as the air flows in and out. Be sure that you are 'belly breathing'—that is, your belly should be moving in and out as you breathe.

After about a minute or two of concentrating on your breathing, start counting sequentially from one to ten on your inhalations and saying to yourself, 'relax' as you exhale. For example, on the first inhalation, say 'one' and see the number one in your mind. On exhalation, say 'relax' and see the word r-e-l-a-x-x-x . . . in your mind. Continue the counting process until you feel quiet and your mind is focused and undisturbed by fleeting thoughts.

The counting process is actually a convenient way to prevent extraneous thoughts and ideas from entering your mind and disturbing you. If your mind is actively occupied with the sights and sounds of the number sequence followed by the word 'relax', then it will be difficult for other thoughts to distract you. Ultimately, just saying the word 'relax' will evoke the relaxation response in you, but for the present it will be necessary to go beyond this level.

FOCUS YOUR ATTENTION

Focusing your attention might sound easy, but it can be quite difficult, especially if you have a very active mind. The counting series described in the previous step is a start, but you will want to go further to experience the deepest possible effects of relaxation. Try the following scene or one of your own choice. Make the scene as real as possible, experiencing as many of the sensual aspects as you can.

South Pacific island beach

I have gone on a holiday to a remote South Pacific island where all my needs are catered for. Today, I have walked to a distant beach, far removed from any habitation. I am standing at the back of the beach in the shade of some palm trees. I can hear the chirping of some birds overhead and can hear the rustling of the palm fronds as they move in the gentle wind. Looking out across the golden-white sands of the beach, I can see the blue-green water of the ocean. Further out to sea, the water becomes a rich, intense blue and then terminates in the arc of the horizon. Overhead, one large, puffy white cloud drifts lazily across the sky from right to left.

As the day is warm, I decide to go down to the water. My feet make contact with the sand and I am immediately aware of the lovely warmth. I can feel the warmth radiating up through the soles of my feet into my legs . . . my abdomen . . . my chest . . . arms . . . neck . . . and head. So warm, so pleasant. As I walk, almost in slow motion down to the water, I can feel the powdery, soft sand slowly giving way under my feet. The sand is very soft and very fine.

I come to the smooth, cool sand, left damp by the receding tide. The sand is firm but my feet leave their prints as I walk. I approach the water's edge and then proceed into the water to calf-depth. The water is cool and very refreshing. I look down into the crystalline clear water and can see on the bottom several fragments of broken shell and a large starfish with purple and blue markings on its upper surface. I can see two small crabs scurrying away from me and a small school of silvery fish darting hither and thither. The water is so clean and clear that I scoop up several handfuls and splash it over my body. Very cool and refreshing.

I now walk back up on to the dry sand and stretch out on my beach towel, face upwards. I can feel the penetrating warmth of the sand working its way up into my back. I can feel droplets of water slowly running off the upper surface of my body. The sun warms and dries my body. So warm . . . So pleasant . . . Lying on the beach, I can only hear the gentle lapping of the waves upon the sand. Occasionally, a seagull calls as it flies overhead, but apart from these sounds, it is blissfully quiet. So quiet, so calm . . . so relaxing . . .

Before going on to the next step of the relaxation procedure, it is important to present still another way of concentrating attention, especially for those who experience difficulty in forming strong visual images.

The script which follows is a progressive muscle relaxation series. All you are asked to do is to focus upon the muscles mentioned and allow them to release as much tension as possible. It might be helpful to allow the muscles to become loose, flabby, warm or even heavy—any state which you feel is associated with relaxation. Read through the script several times and, when you have put it into practice, pause for about fifteen seconds at each muscle group to allow the muscles to relax.

Progressive muscle relaxation

Focus upon your forehead muscles, just above your eyebrows. Feel them become loose . . . warm . . . heavy . . . and relaxed. Now down to your eyebrows . . . very relaxed. Your cheeks and mouth muscles . . . very loose . . . very relaxed. Your jaw muscles . . . nice and loose, letting your lower jaw drop open if you wish. Now your neck muscles, front and back; letting them become warm . . . loose . . . and very relaxed. Now let your shoulders drop as much as you want . . . Notice how good it feels to let that tension go.

Now relax your arms, both of them together. Feel the tension flowing in waves down your arms and out through your fingers. Your arms feel more loose and relaxed with each breath out.

Now your back muscles. Feel them sinking down . . . and down into the chair . . . Just further and further down . . . down . . . down . . . More and more relaxed . . . Now focus upon your chest muscles. Feel them become looser and more relaxed with each breath out. That's it, very relaxed. And now, your abdominal muscles. Letting the tension go, more and more with each breath out. Very relaxed . . . warm and relaxed. And finally, your legs. Just let the tension flow down and away, leaving your legs very loose . . . very relaxed. That's it, very relaxed.

And now, the entire body. Letting the muscle tension go. Feeling very relaxed. Very . . . very re-la-x-x-x-x-ed. Quiet . . . calm . . . and . . . relax-x-x-ed.

If you are still with me, I should add just one more attention-focusing technique, so that you have a range from which to select. One of the major reasons why rigid and inflexible relaxation programs fail is that the user becomes bored. The more variety you can put into your relaxation practice, the greater your motivation to continue practising is likely to be.

Walking down to your relaxation room

Imagine yourself at the top of a lovely curving staircase. You can see the carpet flowing down and around to the left. You can feel the deep pile of the soft carpet under your bare feet. Your hand is resting upon a smooth wooden bannister. As you descend the stairs, one at a time, you will find yourself feeling more and more relaxed with each step down.

Starting at the top, the twentieth step, you step down to 19 . . . now down to 18 . . . letting your hand slide down the bannister as you go . . . 17 . . . more relaxed with each step down . . . 16 . . . 15 . . . 14 . . . 13 . . . feeling the soft carpet under your feet . . . 12 . . . 11 . . . 10 . . . relaxed, more and more relaxed . . . 9 . . . 8 . . . 7 . . . more relaxed with each breath out . . . 6 . . . 5 . . . 4 . . . very relaxed now, very relaxed . . . 3 . . . 2 . . . and now, down to 1 . . . very, very relaxed.

On the far side of the landing at the bottom of the stairs you see a large, very thick door which leads into your private room. You walk over to the door and take hold of the handle and swing it open gently. You walk into the room, pulling the door shut behind you. As you shut the door, you leave all of your problems, worries, cares and concerns outside. Inside your private room, you are free from these concerns.

You look about you and notice the lighting in the room. It is your own room and decorated to your own liking. Take note of the colours on the walls and furnishings and survey the range of furniture. Finally, note the carpet or floor coverings.

You walk over to the most comfortable chair or couch and stretch out, sinking down into the cushions. Almost feeling yourself moving down . . . down . . . down into the cushions. The room is so quiet and so relaxing . . . very relaxing. No cares, problems, worries or concerns. Just you. Very peaceful. Very quiet and so . . . so relaxed.

Having dealt with a few focusing techniques, we are now ready to move on. At this point, it might help if you did some running on the spot to get yourself back into an alert and receptive state. If you were reading the focusing passages to attain a state of relaxation, then delete the running and enjoy your relaxed state.

POSITIVE SELF-SUGGESTIONS

The use of positive self-suggestion is a very important part of preparing for examinations. When you are relaxed, you will note that your body has slowed down. Your heart rate will be slower, your breathing rate will be slower; in fact, most of your bodily functions will be pleasantly slow and easy. Even your mind will be less active, although still aware of what is happening. When your mind is relatively quiet and calm, you can present constructive messages to yourself. While the exact mechanism is unclear, these messages are received and registered by the mind and they can act to positively affect your examination preparation and performance.

It is very important to say here and now that using positive self-messages in the absence of any real work and study for your exams will result in a very comfortable failure. That is, the practice of relaxing yourself and feeding yourself unrealistically positive messages is not going to produce a magical pass. The procedure is best used to enhance your examination preparation. There is simply no substitute for early and regular revision for examinations.

Try using some of the suggestions below while you are deeply relaxed:

- I can relax.
- I can control my mind.
- I can concentrate upon my studies.
- I can perform to the best of my ability.

You will note that the suggestions are all 'I can' type statements. They are fairly general in their scope and are concisely stated. It would be a waste of our time to feed in patently unrealistic messages.

COME BACK SLOWLY

In order to come out of your relaxed state, count slowly from one to five, feeling yourself becoming more alert with each number. At five, slowly open your eyes and then stretch your arms and legs. Do not get straight up on to your feet, as you might become light-headed.

NOTE HOW YOU FEEL

Before doing anything else, notice how relaxed you feel. You might feel a sensation of heaviness in your limbs, or perhaps a feeling of dryness in your mouth. You might feel lethargic and reluctant to move. Take a minute or so and just enjoy that relaxed and comfortable feeling.

PLAN YOUR NEXT RELAXATION SESSION

While the positive effects of your present relaxation experience are still with you, take time to plan when you will next practise your relaxation skills. Remember, practice is absolutely essential and an organised approach is necessary to learn the skill. After a few weeks of practice, you will probably find that the effects of the relaxation experience are so positive that you are actually looking forward to your next practice session.

It is important to mention that you should be planning to practise on average twice a day for about ten to fifteen minutes each time over a three to four-month period in order to make relaxation part of your daily routine and a permanent skill. After you have fully learned how to relax, you could go for prolonged periods without relaxing (not that this is recommended) and return to the practice sessions with little or no difficulty. Learning how to relax is much like learning any other skill—such as riding a bicycle or typing—once learned, the skills are never forgotten. They can be reactivated with little effort at a later time. So, work hard over the next three to four months to firmly establish your lifetime investment in this important skill.

FILL IN A DAILY PRACTICE CHART

As a reminder to carry out your relaxation practice, keep a chart of your daily practice sessions. Rule up a bar graph similar to the one on the following page and before going to bed each night, fill in the boxes for your two sessions of relaxation, if you did carry out the two sessions that day. If you did only one, then obviously fill in only one box, but try to put in three sessions the following day so you can maintain the average of two per day. Before long, you will see a very impressive row of ticks across the page, indicating completed practice sessions. Just seeing the ticks on your chart will provide some strong reinforcement to keep the practice sessions going.

There is strong evidence that suggests that record keeping is a positive reinforcer of new behaviours, so get started with your black pen and keep the practice sessions going. Before long, you will be able to say to yourself, 'relax', and you will feel almost immediately a noticeable decrease in your tension state. Imagine how helpful that will be during your next series of examinations.

Summary

Relaxation is a vital skill, especially if you have been very severely anxious in examinations and hope to survive and thrive in the future. Practise the exercises described in this chapter twice each day and after three months you will be able to push anxiety from your mind and replace it with a very calm and comfortable feeling. That is a much more productive state when taking examinations.

Relaxation training record sheet

Post this record sheet where you will see it every day (e.g. bathroom mirror) and record on it the number of practice sessions you have carried out each day. Fill in the two boxes daily to represent completed practice. Should you miss a day of practice, schedule three make-up sessions over the next two days, aiming to complete 60 practice sessions each month.

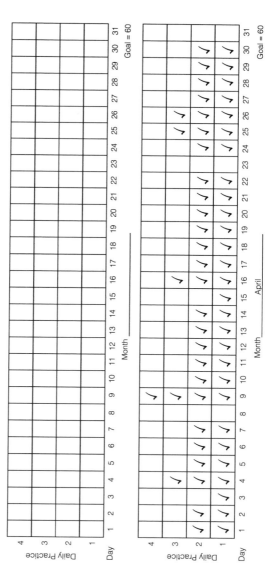

7

Dealing with exam fear

'I'm not really fearful in exams, as long as I know all of the answers beforehand.' — Optimistic student

Probably the most commonly reported psychological concern among secondary and tertiary students is fear of examinations. That's perfectly understandable. Very few of us like to be assessed, especially if there is some possibility that we might perform poorly or even fail. Given our increasingly competitive world, with academic results being one very important criterion for advanced study programs or getting a good job, most students feel under high pressure to perform very well. If they feel that they might fall short of their preferred mark, then fear can be a significant problem.

While fear is not generally a welcome emotion, one redeeming fact is that it is relatively easily treated. Controlled studies have shown that some students report high levels of exam fear even though they have been well prepared for their exams. These students have reported

major problems prior to and during actual exams, including symptoms such as nausea (in one case projectile vomiting in the exam room!), muscle cramping and having mental blocks. The controlled clinical studies conducted with students with these problems have reliably demonstrated vastly improved exam results—in some cases, improvement by up to 30 per cent in their exam performance following treatment.

As an example of how this process can help, it might be interesting to look at the case of Chris, who complained of long-standing and severe examination fear.

CHRIS—FEARFUL IN EXAMS, LOSING MAJOR MARKS

Chris was a second year electrical engineering student who had failed several of his first year subjects. He reported that he had feared all examinations since the beginning of secondary school, but that he did not realise anything could be done about it. A friend of his referred him to the Counselling Service for help.

Preparation was not a problem for Chris. He was very bright and very conscientious. He knew his notes and other study materials very well, but when he walked into the exam room, he was very prone to feeling ill, to the extent of having to leave some exams early. His nausea was often associated with mental blocks. What was really frustrating was that soon after leaving the exam room, he could sit down and work his way through the exam questions with very little difficulty and very good results—but this performance did not count.

Chris was treated with systematic desensitisation (SD), a complicated name for a relatively simple process. Basically, Chris was asked to practise the relaxation technique described in the previous chapter. Once he was well under way with the relaxation, he worked his way through a series of examination scenes which were arranged from low to high anxiety. He practised seeing himself in these scenes but replaced anxiety with relaxation. As a result of his treatment, Chris was able to pass every subject (and several at distinction level) in second year.

THE RATIONALE FOR SYSTEMATIC DESENSITISATION

Our bodies can respond quite strongly to scenes we imagine. The ability to respond so strongly can be used to *reduce* the fear associated with examinations. By practising your relaxation response, you can develop a sufficiently strong relaxation effect which will then counteract the examination fear symptoms. SD is the process by which fear responses are systematically replaced by relaxation. It is important to mention that SD alone will not produce high results. You must be well prepared mentally so that the SD procedure can then handle your emotional responses to the examination situation.

In order to experience some indication of what anxiety and fear in the exam room can be like, have a friend read the following description to you. Try to imagine yourself in the scene as vividly as possible.

Exam room scene

> *You have just arrived for your most difficult examination of the year and you can see other students flicking through their notes and chatting nervously. You can feel the brittle tension in the air. A classmate dashes up and blurts: 'Did you study the Hopkins chapter on the reading list!?' Your mind immediately goes into overdrive: 'Have I overlooked that reading? What if there are questions on it in the exam? Whose notes can I borrow to have a quick browse?'*
>
> *Just as you are scanning the crowd, the doors of the examination room are opened and the students start filing in. You enter the room still thinking about that Hopkins chapter and the possibility of a related exam question. You take a seat as a supervisor announces: 'Do not open your examination booklets until instructed to do so!'*
>
> *You arrange your pens on the desk top and read the graffiti messages on its wooden surface. You look up nervously and see the supervisors canvassing the room with their stern eyes. Not a smile in sight. The chief supervisor then announces: 'You have three hours to complete this examination. Open your examination booklet and begin.'*

Having imagined yourself in the examination room, take note of your heart and breathing rates. If you were able to make the imagery quite real, you might find that your heart rate is accelerated and that you are breathing more rapidly as well.

USING SYSTEMATIC DESENSITISATION

As suggested above, SD will help you to reduce the anxiety experienced in examinations. The process is somewhat similar to overcoming the nervousness which a novice swimmer might experience at the thought or act of going into deep water.

In order to overcome the fear of deep water, the swimmer could construct several stages. For example, simply walking along the beach next to the water should present little difficulty. The next step might be walking in calf-deep water, followed by thigh-deep, waist-deep, chest-deep and then floating. While at each step, the novice swimmer should pause, move about and become adjusted to the present situation until there was no fear or nervousness at being at that particular depth. Then, and only then, would the swimmer advance to the next step. Of course, the swimmer would be very well advised to practise the various swimming strokes and breathing techniques so that there would be no danger of drowning once deep water was reached.

The very same process can be carried out for examination fear. The steps could be constructed along a time dimension instead of space, as was the case in the example above.

Think back to your previous examinations. When did you first notice that you were becoming nervous? At the door of the examination room? The night before? Two weeks before? Or even on day one of the year?

For most examination candidates, thinking about day one of the course would create very little exam fear. We want a very low anxiety level to start, so why not choose day one as the first step of the hierarchy (in this case a series of chronological steps with increasing anxiety as the exam day approaches).

For each step, write a brief description which is as close as possible to your own situation. You might write the notes on small cards, one note per card. When all the cards have been made, sort through them and arrange them in increasing order of anxiety. In order to help you with this ordering, give each card a rating of one to ten, with one being minimal distress and ten being maximal.

The official term for these ratings is SUDS or Specific Units of Distress.

With your rank-ordered cards, you can now use them one at a time to bring to mind imagery relevant to each step. This is done while you are comfortably relaxed, with the cards lying by your side or on your chest. You simply relax thoroughly and then read the first card and imagine the scene in as much detail as possible. When you are able to experience complete relaxation while visualising the scene, then you take the next card, read it and then imagine the setting. In like fashion, you move up the hierarchy until you are able to imagine with complete, or almost complete, relaxation the scene which originally prompted the highest anxiety response.

Let's consider a few examples.

Card 1

Day one of the course, and everyone is comparing timetables and talking about the subjects they're doing. Jill, one of my classmates and a particularly good student, mentions how difficult the exams are in this course. I am standing outside the room where my exams will be held in four months. I can see the empty desks in the room and the blackboard at the front of the room. There is an electric clock on the far wall which will time the exam.

Card 2

One month before the exams. I'm sitting at my desk in my room looking at the list of outstanding assignments and thinking about my revision for the exams. Four weeks to go and still so much to do!

You will notice that in the first two cards a considerable time span has elapsed, from day one of the course to one month before the examinations. It is important for you to construct your own hierarchy to fit your own circumstances. Perhaps you need another step or two to bridge what might be too great a gap. Examination fear usually increases as the date of the exams approaches. Thus, you might need quite a few cards to represent the final week before the exams begin.

It is also worth noting that two different locations were chosen for the first two cards, one in a classroom and the second at the student's desk. Many people who experience examination anxiety report that the fear is strongest at certain times (generally, in the day and weeks just prior to the exams), in certain places (classrooms, laboratories or other places associated with assessments) and with certain people (teaching staff and some classmates—especially those who are always asking how you are going in your preparation).

When constructing your cards, try to incorporate many of the specific factors which contribute to your own anxiety responses. If you are uncertain about what makes you anxious and nervous before an examination, talk with a friend and share your ideas. It is often the case that sharing feelings and thoughts like this will help to sort out uncertainties in your own mind.

Some other cards which might give you some ideas:

Card 3

Two weeks before the exams, and my English lecturer is talking about the major topics which should be revised very thoroughly for the coming exams. My mind is racing back to some of these topics which at the moment seem very foggy. There is a hushed silence in the class.

Card 4

One week before my exams begin. I am looking over the exam schedule on the noticeboard and Jim comes up and cheerily announces that the exams are not worth worrying about!! My exam schedule shows five exams over eight days, with two on day six of the series. Jim is still laughing and joking with some other classmates. Somehow, I miss the joke.

Card 5

> *The morning of my third exam and I'm walking up the stairs to the exam room. There is a lot of nervous chatter going on among the other students. My mind is racing through the topics which I think will appear on the exam. I approach the door of the exam room . . .*

The five sample cards should give you the general idea of how to construct your own hierarchy. Prepare about ten cards and then rank them according to their SUDS level. Arrange the cards in sequence from low to high and then begin the process of desensitisation.

DESENSITISING YOUR FEAR USING RELAXATION AND SD

As SD is a very important and successful method for overcoming exam fear, it is worthwhile elaborating on certain steps in the process.

- When you have relaxed yourself thoroughly, read the first card in the sequence—the one with the lowest SUDS rating.
- Use your imagination to make the scene as realistic as possible. For example, if the scene is set in your room at home, glance around in your imagination and 'see' the furniture, the colour of the walls, any pictures or other fixtures which stand out. In your imagination, sit down at your desk and feel the chair supporting your back and your legs. If it's summer and there's a fan on, listen to its sound and feel the puffs of air blowing against your face when the fan blows in your direction. Are there any background sounds which you can hear? Radio? TV?
- Proceed through the series of cards one at a time.

- If, at any point while imagining a scene, you feel yourself becoming anxious, say 'Stop!' to yourself and picture a stop sign in your mind. The 'stop' command will interrupt the scene which is causing the anxiety.
- Take a comfortable deep breath and say 'relax' to yourself as you exhale to re-establish a relaxation response. Allow as much of the tension and anxiety to flow out as you breathe out. Continue saying 'relax' as you breathe out until you feel thoroughly relaxed.
- Repeat the scene, experiencing the same details as you did previously. If you again experience feelings of nervousness and tension, repeat the 'stop' command and then relax yourself.
- Keep repeating the scene until you can maintain the scene in your mind for about fifteen seconds while still being relaxed.
- When you have reached the point where you can maintain the scene in your mind for fifteen seconds while being relaxed, advance to the next card and repeat the process.
- If one or more scenes prove to be particularly difficult, carry the relevant cards with you during the day. When you have a few spare moments, imagine yourself in one of the scenes and say 'relax' as you breathe out. By imagining the difficult scenes over and over, you can progressively desensitise yourself to the anxiety associated with those scenes.
- By the time you have successfully worked your way through the entire hierarchy, you will find that you can relax even under the most difficult exam conditions. The secret is to pair the relaxation response which has already been associated with the word 'relax' to the various scenes. The process might take several weeks, but the activity (or more aptly put, the lack of activity) is quite pleasant and enjoyable.
- If you do not have weeks or even days to work through your hierarchy in a relaxed fashion, you can

still benefit from spending a few minutes each hour imagining your hierarchy scenes. Carry the cards with you and get relaxed when and where you can. Imagine one scene at a time and say 'relax' as you exhale. This massed practice approach is not as good as the spaced practice, but it is better than going into an exam in a tight knot.

Systematic desensitisation is much like taking a vaccine. You expose yourself to safe levels of examination stress by using realistic imagination. If you practise over a period of time, you can achieve a very positive response.

In essence, you can take much of the fear out of your exam experiences by starting your revision early, revising your notes frequently and well, learning how to relax and by using SD. Be certain that you start your preparation *early*, so that you have sufficient time to master these tasks.

The purpose of starting to learn how to relax months before the exams is to ensure that when they arrive, you will be able to put into practice the vital skills for exam success. You will quickly realise that an exam room is not the conventional place to stretch out and practise your full relaxation response. However, the trained relaxer *can* call up a brief but effective relaxation response when the stress level gets too high during the exam. The next section describes how to use your relaxation response during the actual exam process.

RELAXING QUICKLY DURING EXAMINATIONS

For students who habitually have problems with strong fear in exams, there are many advantages in being able to relax quickly, even during ongoing exams.

There are at least three reasons why being able to relax quickly in an exam will benefit you. One, you are likely to be more comfortable, given that examination rooms are not generally designed with comfort in mind. Two, you can prevent muscle cramps. Writer's cramp is a common problem when the muscles of the writing hand are being pushed to their limits. Three, working with a relatively relaxed mind will promote more flexible thinking. You should be able to bend and flex your memory to its maximum, but still keep your mental systems organised.

Having stated what is likely to be obvious to many experienced exam candidates, what can the fear-prone person do in an examination to maintain a relaxed and flexible approach?

Keeping (relatively) relaxed in exams

- Periodically, close your eyes and take a comfortably deep breath and then let the air out, slowly and quietly. As you breathe out, say 'relax' to yourself and feel the tension flowing out of your body.
- While relaxing during the deep breath, allow your arms and hands to dangle at your sides. Feel the warmth from your blood flow into your hands. Imagine the tension flowing out through your fingertips.
- Flex and relax your finger muscles several times to promote blood flow.
- Change your body position slightly to allow more blood flow to your thighs, buttocks and back. Make the movements slowly and gently so as not to disturb your neighbours.
- Stretch your arms, legs and back.
- Take another slow and deep breath and say 'relax' as you breathe out and then return to your work on the examination.

The entire process of breathing, dangling, flexing, changing, stretching and breathing again can be done in about 30 seconds or less. The benefits to be derived from the periodic relaxation break make the time investment very worthwhile. In order to experience the feel of the process, why not try the steps right now? Practice is the key to a better performance.

SUMMARY

Systematic desensitisation (SD) is a process which will help you to reduce exam fear. Having attained a good relaxation response, imagine exam preparation and performance scenes so that your relaxation response becomes associated with these imagined events. The process will take several months to complete, so start early. Students who have previously been affected severely by exam fear have reported up to 30 per cent improvement in their exam results—so doing it is very worthwhile.

8

Organising your revision

'I've got plenty of time for revision! Just be sure to wake me at 7.00 am for the 9.00 am exam.' — Even more optimistic student

This will be a very focused and short chapter, as you may be reading it with very little time available before your exams. If that is the case, then scan the sections and pick out the major themes which will be of immediate use to you. Having done that, get back to your own books and notes and make every minute count. You will not be examined on the contents of this chapter, but you will certainly have to know your class notes.

JULIE—LAST-MINUTE PREPARATION, FRANTIC AND FURIOUS

Julie was a second year Arts student who had always left her preparation until the night before her exams. She fully recognised the fact that she was a procrastinator, but her approach had always produced sufficiently good results so

far and she couldn't see why she should change. However, the tide was turning.

In her second semester of second year, she found her subjects were getting much more complicated and the notes more voluminous. She was questioning whether her old last-minute preparation pattern would be sufficient and thus sought advice from the Counselling Service four days before her exams were to start. Based upon her reports and the size of her note folders, I could easily see that unless she had a photographic memory, she was going to be hard-pressed to get through that work load in time for her exams.

There was no denying that Julie was bright and capable, but there was a limit (usually defined by time) to how much she could get done. We mapped out a daily revision plan with dedicated time to a systematic, but hasty, review of each of her four subjects plus time to wrap up the remaining two assignments. The remaining days were going to be very long and very busy, but Julie was committed to the challenge.

When she returned after the semester break, Julie reported that she was just able to pass each of her four subjects in first semester. Her borderline passes shocked her into the reality that she must plan ahead and get started on her exam revision weeks, not days, before the exams. She realised that her eleventh hour approach had reached its limit and new approaches were now necessary. With a fair amount of perseverance, she was able to discipline herself into preparing earlier for her exams during the remainder of her degree.

Whether or not you have planned ahead, let's assume that you have about five or six weeks before your exams for a systematic revision. Yes, that's an ideal, but given the importance of exams, the closer that the ideal and the real can come together, the better for you and your results. The general plan of attack for your revision is to consult your syllabi (the topics, schedule and exam information available for each of your subjects), plan your time and accommodate any special problems or needs. Let's look at each of these issues.

CONSULT YOUR SUBJECT SYLLABI

The syllabus for any one subject will contain the lecture topics and presentation schedule for the semester. The syllabus should also contain information about your tests and exams and any assignments (essays, reports, tutorial papers and projects). By reading over your syllabus, you should be able to derive a very clear idea about the essential topics which the teaching staff felt you should know. If you are unclear about the major issues, ask your teachers. If they feel it is inappropriate to provide any further information, they will tell you so, but there is no harm in asking relevant questions about your assessments. The important point here is that you should be as focused and informed as possible on the major issues to be revised, especially if time is very limited.

PLAN YOUR TIME AND REVISION SCHEDULE

With the major topics clearly in mind, next set up a revision schedule. You should go through your notes, books and any other materials as many times as possible. Too many students walk into their major exams with a 'once or twice' preparation—that is, they've read through their notes. They may be vaguely familiar with the topics, but when the crunch comes in the exam room, this level of preparation will be generally inadequate. For best results, you should have enough time to go through your notes and other materials at least four to five times. That might sound like Utopia, but with forward planning and careful use of your time, it is possible.

In order to get the most value out of your study time, first organise your revision on several different time plans. Work out a weekly study plan for each of the final weeks, a daily plan for each day and finally, a study plan for the next few hours. With these three time plans, you can see how each day's progress relates to your overall task. Every hour counts—in fact, every minute is important. A quick glance at your current 'battle plan' will reinforce the necessity to keep focused and driving ahead with your revision.

The second step is to divide your study tasks into the available time. Let's say, for example, that you have four examinations of equal importance and you want to go through your notes and other materials in each subject about five times during the next six weeks. On a sheet of

Pre-Exam Period Planner

Subj.	Wk. 1	Wk. 2	Wk. 3	Wk. 4	Wk. 5	Wk. 6	Exam
A	Rev'n 1		Rev'n 1	Rev'n 2	Rev'n 3	Rev'n 4	Exam
B	R1	R2	R3	R4	R5		Exam
C		R1		R2	R3	R4 R5	Exam
D			R1		R2	R3 R4	Exam

paper, rule off six vertical columns, one for each week. On the left-hand margin, list vertically the four subjects you will be revising. Draw an arrow for each subject across the weeks columns to the point where you plan to have completed the first revision of your notes. The goals might differ depending upon the amount of material to be covered and the difficulty of the subject. Count on the first revision taking much more time than the subsequent revisions. The fifth or sixth run through your notes might only take an hour or so—perhaps on the morning of the examination.

You will notice from the chart above that subjects A and B have been allocated relatively brief first revision periods compared to subjects C and D. The important feature of the chart is that you give sufficient time to the first revision of the difficult subjects, while still having enough time to go through the notes of your other subjects. Time is certainly limited and you will have to be very careful about how you are using it. Remember, the major objective is to go through your notes several times (up to four or five times for maximum confidence) before you enter the exam room.

Most students know when they function at peak effectiveness. Some people are morning workers while others find they are more effective in the evening or at night. Given that you are probably going to be studying at any available hour during those final weeks before your exams, you might want to consider what subjects you will be studying in your high and low periods. Rather than plan too far in advance, take each day as it comes and spend some time at the beginning to organise your day's work. Your mood on that day can be a factor that might well affect your study program. If you are feeling down, then start with one of your favourite subjects to get you going. When you have developed some momentum, then schedule one of your least favourite subjects. Be flexible and adaptable, but keep the revision process moving ahead.

If your time is very limited, say five or fewer days, then you may need to cut your losses and put your time where the most marks can be earned. That is, concentrate on knowing well the material which is: (a) important in the course, and (b) not hard to understand. You may have to be very selective in your approach and ignore particularly difficult topics. Keep asking yourself where you are most likely to score the most marks as a guide about what to do next.

Tool box for time management and exam revision

In order to make the most use of your time and revision possibilities, here are some 'tools' which might be helpful.

- *Flash cards* As mentioned earlier in this book, you can study on the run by using palm-sized flash cards. Write the topic on one side and any important details on the reverse side. Carry them with you every day and revise during any of those many different waiting, and usually wasted, short periods of time every day.
- *Self-adhesive notes* Write critical topics and any other exam-relevant notes on these and then place

them on door handles, windows, computer screen and other often-looked-at places. The recurring words and themes should stick in your mind as well as they stick to the walls.

- *Alarm clock for frequent study breaks* Intense revision is mentally very tiring, so be certain to take frequent but short study breaks. In order to ensure that you get back to your desk on time, set an alarm clock or the oven timer for the appropriate time, and when the buzzer goes off, get back to work!
- *Highlighters and coloured pens* Make your revision notes as colourful as possible. The more creative you can be and the more colourful your notes become, the greater the chance of good recall in the exam room.
- *Punching bag for frayed nerves and aggressive tendencies* Far better to bash a bag than to hit walls (especially brick ones) or, heaven forbid, hit people. However, when tensions are very high, these tendencies can emerge, so head for the gym or pound your pillow. A few good jabs, hooks and uppercuts will make you feel much better.

SPECIAL PROBLEMS AND NEEDS

One of the chief problems faced by students on the downhill run into the exam room (no matter how much time exists before the dreaded event) is that all the material in their notes looks very examinable. How do you separate the wheat from the chaff?

Use the Rule of 3

As you revise each section of your notes, ask yourself, 'If I were the examiner, what are the *three most important concepts* or points in this section which I would want my students to know?'. This basic question might help you to locate issues which are potentially more important as you revise your notes from another perspective—that of your examiner. Having decided which three points are the most important in that section, make a brief note of them and move on to the next section. Having revised all sections of your notes, then go back and work intensively upon the groups of three items per section.

Confer with classmates about the most examinable items

The same process as noted above can be used with a small and disciplined group of classmates. You stand to get more helpful information from the pooled ideas of the group members than from just your own thoughts. But be careful about losing control and focus. If you are working with a student group shortly before your exam period starts, then nerves will be tingling and disciplined discussion might be difficult.

CUSTOMISE YOUR REVISION APPROACH

Another important issue which confronts most students is—what differences in approach should I use for Arts/social science subjects as opposed to maths/science and engineering subjects? Clearly, these are very different types of subjects and their differences warrant individual study tactics.

For the Arts and social science subjects, you will be mostly dealing with broad concepts and topics and many divergent themes, theories and theorists. Your major job will be to know these main issues very well. Look over your syllabi and pick out the topics which have been the focus of lectures, class discussions and any special projects. Go over these topics many times so that you know them very well. The one advantage you have, especially if you will be examined by essay questions, is that you will be able to describe and discuss the topics, as opposed to solving a problem which is likely to have only one right answer.

The maths/science and engineering students have a relatively more difficult challenge in that they have to know everything from the general to the very specific. Theories, theorists, concepts and issues are just as important as the facts and figures and problem solutions. If your subject is mostly problem oriented and you will be expected to produce answers to problems during the exam, then you need to prepare by solving many, many practice problems beforehand. As you can guess, practising problem solutions is best done on a week-to-week basis, as there will not be sufficient time in the final few weeks to handle problems from the entire semester or year. In addition to the problems for the maths, science and engineering students, you will also need to revise your laboratory work very carefully. Don't forget the statistical procedures and data analyses as they might be presented as problems in the exam.

EXPECTATIONS ABOUT REVISION AND RECALL

Revising for exams is a difficult and demanding process. A good deal of the frustration comes from the feeling of personal incompetence when you first start going over your notes. It is very important for you to realise that these feelings are perfectly normal and predictable and that they will pass as you become more knowledgeable about your notes. It might be helpful to document the general psychological stages you might experience as you work through your notes.

Revision #1

You feel frightened by the amount of work to be done and the time remaining before your exams begin. Many of the concepts in your notes are familiar in name only—it will take considerable work to understand the background and the details of these potentially examinable topics.

Basically, you might be feeling quite baffled and perhaps even fearful.

Revision #2

Time is still a major worry. You are going through your notes and they are becoming more familiar but certainly not firmly understood at this stage. Your attention may be distracted by thoughts about how little you know and how soon you will be examined.

Revision #3

You are now beginning to feel slightly more comfortable as you can recite most of the topics and their subheadings. However, there may still be some important gaps, which are a concern. The revision at this stage is going much more quickly which is reassuring.

Revision #4

The topics now are reasonably clear and understood. The revision process is going quite quickly and you can press on through your notes with a fair degree of certainty and clarity. However, some fine details here and there may need further attention.

Revision #5

Most of you now feel quite certain of your knowledge. You can almost see in your mind the topics as they are represented on your note pages. You can discuss the topics with confidence and you are now feeling more confident of your ability to deal with the exam questions.

Note that the final stage was prefaced with 'Most of you', as there will be some who will feel unsettled and uncertain no matter how many times they have gone through their notes. If you are one of the constant worriers, then try to accept the fact that you have prepared well and that you know the material. Yes, there could be some difficult questions which will test and try your potentials, but the same is true for every other student in the class. If this reassurance is not sufficient to calm your nerves, then see a student counsellor for some help with exam anxiety—well before your exams are due to start.

MANAGE YOUR BODY, MOODS AND RELATIONSHIPS

You might have a brief wait before being able to see a student counsellor during the lead-up period to the exams (peak period), so here are a few self-help tips for coping with your nerves.

- *Take care with too much caffeine* Your liver can only detoxify about 500 mg per day—that's about three to five level teaspoons of freeze-dried instant regular coffee. Your adrenalin levels will already be in full production, so you don't really need additional stimulation.
- *Try to get a good night of sleep each night in the week leading up to your exams* You will need to be well rested in order to deal well with your exams, so don't skimp on your sleep. Do *not* take any stay-awake pills, as some people have follow-on effects the next day which can undermine thinking in the exam room.
- *Eat regularly, but not too much* Once again, you need to be at full pace during your revision and when you enter the exam room. Your brain depends upon a good supply of energy—best found in healthy food—to function well.
- *Expect to feel nervous* Some nervousness is quite normal, but just to put your feelings into perspective, talk with several classmates and see how they are feeling. You'll probably find that they are feeling much the same way.

- *Do some exercise to relieve the anxiety* Pre-exam agitation and jitters are best dealt with by some direct activity, such as going for a short but brisk walk, doing some running on the spot, or some other form of exercise. This will help burn off some of the excess energy and should allow you to then sit down and get on with some productive work.

- *Breathe slowly and say to yourself, 'relax', as you exhale* If you find yourself getting light-headed, keep your breathing rate slow and steady, as there may be a tendency for it to accelerate unduly. If you have been hyperventilating (breathing too quickly in short, shallow breaths), then cup your hands tightly and hold them over your mouth and nose so that you rebreathe your exhaled air. This will help to restore a proper balance of carbon dioxide in your blood and thus assist you in settling down and feeling calmer. Repeat this rebreathing technique whenever necessary.

- *Keep your relationships intact* Your relationships are likely to become a bit tense during exam time. If you are involved in a relationship which has been marginal and on the point of breaking up, be certain *not* to break up just before or during the exam period. Hold on and if the situation does not improve, then consider breaking up *after* the exams are over. The reason is very simple: matters of the heart will certainly affect matters of the mind.

A FEW WORDS ABOUT CRAMMING

Just a few words about the very familiar practice of cramming. Basically, it's best not to cram, but to revise on a regular weekly basis throughout the semester. But, if you must cram, here are a few pointers to make the cramming session as productive as possible.

- Assuming this is a night-before-the-exam effort, start early in the evening when you are still relatively fresh and alert.
- Take frequent but short breaks to maintain some composure.
- Focus on the major issues. There is probably not sufficient time to attack the details.
- Use the 3 Rs: Read, (w)Rite, Recite as you learn the most examinable topics.
- Keep away from coffee and tea. Do not take stimulants or stay awake pills.
- No time for word-by-word reading—skim and scan for the big issues.
- Try to get some sleep, but set at least two alarms, preferably out of arm's reach.

SUMMARY

Being well organised for your revision is generally associated with good exam results. Plan your weeks, days and hours (even minutes!) before your exams and make your study sessions count. Think like an examiner to identify key issues and then go over them four to five times. If cramming has been a habit, break it and start your revision early in the semester.

9

Performing well during the exam period

'Even though I haven't had too much time to prepare, I know it will all come to me when I open up the exam booklet.' — Exam candidate and strong believer in divine inspiration

The long-awaited day has arrived! After much sweat and toil, you will have the opportunity of showing how much (*not* how little!) you know about the topics you have been studying over the past many weeks. With a good breakfast under your belt and plenty of time to arrive at the examination venue, you head off. While on the way, your mind might be entertaining some of the following concerns:

- I hope I can find the right room where the exam is to be held.
- Will I get those panicky feelings again like I did last semester?
- The builders are probably jack-hammering the floor of the room upstairs, like last year.

- Those computerised answer sheets can be a problem, especially getting the black marks in the right spaces.
- I've got to be certain to read the directions more carefully this time—no sense cramming in three essays when only two were asked for.

WAKE UP EARLIER THAN REALLY NECESSARY

If you have studied into the early hours of exam day and have decided to get several hours of sleep, be sure to set *two* alarm clocks. It would be wise to place the clocks at the far side of the room so that you are not able to reach out from bed and turn them off.

For the very heavy sleepers who might be tempted to return to bed 'just for another few minutes', put a basin of water on the floor at the far side of the room near your alarm clocks. When you reach down to turn off the alarms, liberally splash cold water over your face, neck and arms and then stand in the water. Having wet a good proportion of your body, you are less tempted to return to bed.

You certainly do not want to oversleep and run the risk of getting to the exam late or missing it altogether, as either one of these situations can put your results at risk. If you can't trust either the alarms or yourself, then have a family member or housemate wake you on time. You might also consider using the wake-up service of your telephone company. Whatever system you use, you must get up on time.

HAVE SOME BREAKFAST

Too many students dash off to their morning exams without any breakfast. They often say that they are too nervous to eat breakfast, but several hours later, they can regret that decision. Your brain needs energy to think, analyse, plan, solve and write. If you haven't had any food since dinner yesterday, then your blood glucose levels are likely to be very low—hardly the condition for a three-hour, probing examination experience.

If you are concerned about the negative effects of various foods upon you on exam days (indigestion, wind, stomach cramps, etc.), then consult a dietitian for suggestions about various alternatives. It really doesn't matter what types of food you eat, as long as you have sufficient energy reserves to carry you through the exam.

VERIFY THE VENUE

I once made the gross error of assuming that the *provisional* examination timetable posted six weeks before the exam period was good enough. I arrived at the appointed place on time and found no one else there—when about 250 students were due to be examined. At 8.50 am for a 9.00 am examination start, I became *very* concerned about the situation. I dashed around looking for a noticeboard with the timetables and found one with a *final* edition of the timetable. My examination venue had been changed to a room on the opposite side of campus. I sprinted across campus and arrived about ten minutes after the start of the exam—out of breath, sweaty, flustered, and more than mildly angry at myself. However, I was fortunate that the exam time had not been changed to the day before!

Some words to the wise—check and even re-check the dates, times and venues for all your exams just before the start of the exam period. If you are assigned to a venue which is unfamiliar to you, then take the time to find the building and the room before that exam day.

Be aware that rooms do not always run in strict numerical order and that buildings are not always identified by a particular name. These potential problems are easily solved by simply finding the buildings and rooms before the exam period starts.

CHECK THE STARTING TIME

Depending upon the type of examination you are taking, there can be early check-in times prior to the official start of the examination. For particularly large examinations, there might be a specified arrival time which allows for checking-in of the candidates. It may sound unduly complicated and potentially paranoiac, but in some examinations, such as those which qualify candidates to work overseas, the check-in procedure may involve scrutinising passports, checking handwriting specimens, and even fingerprinting. If these latter measures are part of the check-in procedure, then the examination authorities should let you know beforehand so that adequate time is allowed. Once again, your goal is to start your examination with as much calmness, composure and confidence as possible.

CHOOSE YOUR SEAT

As you will be spending up to three, or possibly four hours, sitting in a chair taking your exam, the issue of seating warrants special consideration. On entering the examination room, you will either be assigned a seat or you will be able to select a seat. If the latter is the case, several considerations could be pertinent. First, if you have found that in previous examinations you were distracted by students sitting around you, then select a seat in the front row of the room. While you possibly will have students sitting beside you, the bulk of the students will be behind you. The only problem with sitting at the front is that you could be distracted by the supervisors, who often sit or stand at the front and can be prone to whispering among themselves. Should this happen, do not hesitate to politely ask them not to speak as it is distracting you.

You might also want to take note of the location of students whom you know crack their knuckles or sigh very vocally during exams. Other students to avoid are those who scratch away vigorously with their pens and produce voluminous essays while you are still slaving away on page two. If you are able to choose, find a spot where you are at a safe distance from these problematic classmates.

Having decided whether you prefer a front seat or one somewhere else in the room, you might next consider the temperature factor. If you are taking your exams in the warm months, consider the window locations and the angle of the sun. If the room is already warm, it will become warmer still when there are many students inside. You may therefore wish to avoid seats where you will be bathed in sunshine. If you are assigned a seat in a sunny spot, ask the supervisor if the blinds or shades can be adjusted to prevent discomfort from either the sun's heat or glare.

Just as personal accidents and misadventures seem to occur more frequently on exam days, the council road workers seem also to choose these days to tear up the pavements outside examination rooms. Trying to divert a team of workers from their appointed duty is hopeless. If you have the misfortune to strike this situation, ask the supervisors to close the windows and draw the blinds to reduce the noise level as much as possible. If the noise problem or any other significant distracter continues to be a major concern, be certain to mention this to your exam supervisors, as provision is generally made for them to report any irregularities to the central administration.

FILL IN THE ANSWER SHEET IDENTIFICATION

In examinations where computerised answer sheets are used, time will be allowed at the beginning of the examination for candidates to complete identification grids on the answer sheets. In order to complete this procedure fully, you may be asked to record a registration number—

that is, if pre-registration was necessary to take the exam. Be certain to have your registration slip when you leave home, otherwise there will be some anxious moments when this process starts.

You will certainly have to provide your name and possibly other information, such as the correct name of your academic course, your institutional affiliation, your date of birth, examination centre number and the date. The whole process can be confusing and the matter is not made any easier by having to fill in numeric and alphabetical grids. The major problem to guard against is filling in the wrong column. This problem is more likely to occur in the number grid where many students assume that the number zero is the last number in the vertical columns instead of the first number. Given that you are most likely to be firstly identified by your student or registration number, filling in the wrong number can cause all sorts of difficulties. It is always best to check that you have filled in the correct letters and numbers after you have completed the grids. Should you make a mistake, be certain to completely erase the error and fill in the correct space.

READING TIME

Following the examination check-in and recording of iden-tification details, you might be given a short 'reading period', or time to read the examination questions. During this period, students are generally not allowed to do any writing. A critical step in any examination is reading, and then re-reading the directions. Re-reading these important sections is certainly *not* a waste of time. Many students have ploughed into their examination papers with only a once-over-lightly reading of the directions, and then dis-covered too late that they have made a fundamental error in their approach. The reading time is intended to allow you to read, think and plan your approach to the questions. However, the initial exposure to the questions can produce quite strong reactions in your mind. Imagine yourself reading the first question which deals with an issue you thought was trivial and therefore treated very lightly in your revision. What sorts of feelings are likely to be pulsing through your body? Probably strong fear, if not sheer panic. Many students might become extremely tense and begin to entertain thoughts of impending failure. Before you allow a doomsday attitude to set in, move along to the next question. Here you may find that your preparation has been well rewarded.

Having read the instructions and the examination questions, you can establish your plan of attack. Knowing the number of questions and their focus, and perhaps their different mark value, you can then allocate your time and your priorities.

ALLOCATE YOUR TIME

Allocating your time to the major sections or questions on the paper takes only a minute or two and is a simple task to complete, but many candidates go flying past this critical step. Many of these students are the ones who write notes to the markers in the final minute of the exam: 'I ran out of time and could not complete this question'. Such notes win very little sympathy from markers, and certainly no marks. Part of the examination process is to hold yourself accountable for the way you use your time, so take a minute or two at the start of the examination to get yourself and your time organised.

How do you apportion your time in an examination? As a basic principle, you want to be certain that you obtain credit for the material you know well. You can imagine the frustration of working through the exam questions in their presented order and finding that you do not have enough time to fully complete the last question, an item addressing an area you know particularly well. In order

to prevent this situation from occurring, list the order in which you intend to do the questions at the beginning of the exam. The order should take into account two criteria: your knowledge of the questions and the mark value of the various questions. Having decided how much time you plan to devote to each question, it is up to you to keep to the plan. Remember, it is far better to have something down on paper for each question than have a near perfect answer for one question and empty space for the rest.

Another consideration which might be relevant to your time allocation is your possible preference for essay, short-answer and multiple-choice type questions. Some students have reported that, because they felt they were weak in essay writing, they devoted too much time to the essay part of the examination and consequently did not have enough time to deal with the multiple-choice questions. Once again, be certain that you get credit for your strengths. The following chapter will discuss the different types of examination questions.

One further suggestion about planning your attack relates to fatigue and writer's cramp. If you have the option of writing several essays and completing a series of multiple-choice questions, you might want to do one or two of the essays, switch to the multiple-choice section, and then return to complete the essays. By inserting the multiple-choice section in the middle of your exam, you allow your hand to have a bit more rest. Not only will your hand get a break, but also your mind will benefit by switching from the creative task of essay writing to the more analytical chore of choosing the most correct multiple-choice answer. Generally speaking, giving yourself a change of pace during exams is a good idea. Staying in the same mental gear can result in unnecessary fatigue.

One final point is well worth mentioning. In some large public examinations, there might be restrictions upon going back to previously completed sections. The instructions should clearly specify any such restrictions. Be certain to listen carefully and consider these special conditions when you are planning how to proceed with your examination.

BE NEAT

As noted above, after several hours of writing, your hand can get tired and your handwriting can deteriorate. Look over some of your past exam papers and see if your writing is legible. If your writing is indecipherable (ask a friend to pass judgment), practise writing for long periods to condition your hand muscles. One exercise you might try is to take notes continually during a one-hour current affairs TV program, including any commercials. Your hand muscles will be very tired on your first several attempts, but they will strengthen with practice and the legibility of your handwriting should improve.

Why bother about your handwriting? The reason is very basic, and very important—clear and legible writing can win you marks. Most examination markers have to read paper after paper and if they strike a series of almost unreadable essays, the marker is not likely to be sympathetic to the plight of the fatigued candidate. Make the situation as easy for the marker and as beneficial for yourself as you can.

CHECK YOUR PAPER

Just before the end of the examination, take a few minutes to look over your answers and essays. Correct any spelling errors, insert any missing punctuation and tidy up any blotches or stray marks. If you have used a computerised answer sheet, be certain that your answer marks completely fill the spaces and that you have not left any answer spaces unfilled. If there is no penalty for guessing and you have not completed a section, fill in a particular letter—say, B—for each of the incomplete questions. You might just pick up a few marks in that final minute of the exam.

SUMMARY

Exam day has arrived! Be sure to rise early, eat breakfast and get an early start to the exam venue. Choose (if allowed) the best seat for you and when the reading time starts, carefully plan your strategy. Keep strictly to your allocated times so that all sections of the exam are addressed. Check your paper for errors and neatness before the exam finishes.

10

Dealing with particular types of examinations

'I'm a gambler at heart—it's just a pity that True–False questions are not more common.' — Wishful student

As the examination candidate, you are faced with the daunting task of confronting a variety of different examination formats. You might have to demonstrate your logical reasoning and creative abilities in one or more essay questions; or show how well you can condense a series of logical thoughts into one concise paragraph in a short-answer section; or cope with multiple-choice questions.

A common misconception held by many candidates is that they failed their exams because they did not know the material sufficiently well to pass. Obviously, knowing the material well *is* critical, but another important criterion for passing examinations is the candidate's ability to think and argue in a logical, concise and clear way. Clear and concise expression is more important in essay examinations than in multiple-choice tests. However, you will certainly

have to have a clear and logical mind to work your way through a battery of complex multiple-choice questions.

This chapter will address the major types of examinations, including essays, short answer, multiple choice, true–false and matching. A recent and interesting variation in examination format has been the open-book examination, which is not as easy as it sounds. Finally, the important issue of the laboratory examination will be discussed.

ESSAY EXAMINATIONS

Writing essays under examination conditions has been a traditional method of assessment for more years than most educators want to remember. The assumption behind the essay examination is that sitting in an examination room prodding your brain for clear arguments and convincing evidence for two to three consecutive hours is a valid way to measure your academic merit. This may or may not be so. The reality is, however, that essay examinations are very common and you are well advised to be prepared for them. This section will present some guidelines which will assist you in performing as well as possible in examination essays.

Read and interpret the question carefully

The first and foremost task in answering an essay question is to be certain you understand what is being asked. That might sound simplistic, but hasty reading and misinterpretation of the question have been the undoing of many a candidate. Make sure you understand specifically what is being asked: read the question, then re-read it and then underline the key words.

Underline the key words

The key words in the question are the *topical terms* and *concepts* about which you are being asked to write and the *operational words* which tell you how you are to do it. The following list presents some common operational words found in essay examinations.

Analyse Describe the main ideas and their relationships, assumptions and significance.

Compare Show the pros and cons or the similarities and differences.

Contrast Compare by focusing upon the differences.

Criticise Present your considered opinion based upon the pros and cons. Criticising does not necessarily mean condemning the idea. It is best to present a balanced argument showing both the positive and negative points.

Define Present the meaning of the term, generally in a formalised way. Including an example will enhance your definition.

Describe Present a detailed and accurate picture of the event or phenomenon.

<u>Discuss</u> Describe the event or phenomenon, but give the positive and negative aspects. At university level, it would be fair to expect a critical discussion, citing the significance of the topic and any assumptions, if relevant.

<u>Evaluate</u> Weigh up or give your assessment of the relevant matter, citing positive and negative features, advantages and disadvantages, and so on.

<u>Interpret</u> Present the meaning, using examples and presenting your opinion.

<u>Justify</u> Present the background for a particular event or phenomenon and why you think it is so. You will be expected to present evidence to support your views and conclusions.

<u>Review</u> Present a summary of the important aspects or parts and comment critically where appropriate.

<u>Summarise</u> Present a brief overview of the major points with commentary about why they are important.

<u>Trace</u> Describe the history, development or progress of the event or phenomenon.

Write down your initial ideas

Having read the question and underlined the key words, jot down immediately the ideas which come to your mind. Don't worry about the quality of these ideas, just get them down. The process is similar to brainstorming, a process of getting ideas out, no matter what their quality. It's quantity you want at this stage.

Organise your ideas

After you have brainstormed the essay topic for several minutes, look for central themes or connecting thoughts which relate the ideas to the essay topic. Pay particular attention to the instruction words, such as 'critically discuss', 'evaluate', for example. They will help you to structure your essay.

Let's take an example to help make this point clearer. Imagine that you have been asked the following question in an economics examination: 'Compare and contrast the economic theories of Marx and Keynes, with special reference to the national economic situation over the past two years'. Having jotted down ideas relevant to the theories of Marx and Keynes, choose those which have special relevance to the economic conditions over the past two years. Try to organise your ideas into a simple and logical structure, perhaps using geometric or graphic forms to assist you with the organising.

Outline your essay

Having jotted down your ideas and major points and tried to organise them in a coherent and logical structure, take perhaps five minutes to carry out the next and very important step—writing an outline. In the introductory paragraph, remember that you must introduce the topic and, just as importantly, you must tell the marker how you will be structuring the essay. The succeeding paragraphs should deal with the major points you are trying to establish in your essay. If you are in doubt about what to say, ask yourself what are the three to five most important aspects of the topic being asked and then try to link them together in some kind of relevant structure. Having outlined the introduction and body of the essay, devote a paragraph or two at the end to summarise your argument and present your conclusion. The importance of preparing an outline before you start really addresses the problem of digression, straying from the central theme of the essay. In a time-limited exercise like an examination, it is critical that you plan your essay and then stay on target. Make sure you stick to your time allocation *strictly*.

Write your essay

With an eye on the clock, you are now faced with the task of writing your essay. As specified before, keep to your time schedule so that you can attempt all the questions. When writing your essays, there are several guidelines which might be helpful.

Get directly to the point

In the first paragraph, tell the marker what you are going to say and how you are going to present your argument. The introductory paragraph below might be appropriate for the Marx and Keynes question mentioned earlier:

The theories of Marx and Keynes have continued to have an impact upon current economic conditions. This essay will firstly present a brief synopsis of Keynesian and Marxist theories and then present the positive and negative aspects of each theory, especially as they relate to three current economic phenomena: balance of trade, interest rates variation and inflation. Each of these phenomena will be critically analysed with reference first to Keynesian theory and then to the theory of Marx. The essay will conclude with a statement about which theory appears to have the more practical value for the national economic situation over the past two years.

The marker who reads the introductory paragraph will probably respond with pleasure, relieved that the essay seems to be well-planned and organised. By getting directly to the point and showing the marker how you are going to progress, you are ensuring a favourable and positive impact.

Focus upon the major points you are trying to present

Having introduced your argument and how you are going to handle it, try to deal with each of your major points in one paragraph in the body of your essay. Each point can be presented as the lead sentence of the paragraph and the following sentences can be used to help illustrate or amplify the point.

Use transitional linking phrases

To help the marker follow your presentation and argument, it is useful to employ transitional linking phrases to make your essay flow more smoothly. The transitional links can also serve as guideposts, telling the marker what you have completed and where you are going next.

Take, for example, the following part of a sentence midway in your essay: 'Having considered the current economic phenomena, foreign trade balance and interest rate variations, the present inflationary situation can be regarded as . . .'. The transitional phrase at the start of this sentence tells the reader that you have completed your first two points and that you are now progressing to your third point. By using these transitional phrases, you make the marker's job easier—and, the easier you make the work for the marker, the better you are likely to fare in the examination.

Use the marker's language

As suggested earlier, your marks will not only depend upon how much you know, but also upon how you present your essay. The concern about your presentation style can be focused upon several levels of your essay: at the overall organisation of your essay; at the structure of your paragraphs; and even down to the level of the actual words you choose in your sentences. Does that sound too pedantic? Perhaps, but ask any successful advertising person and they will confirm the importance of language in marketing a product—in the present case, you are trying to market the content of your essay.

One strategy respected by most experienced salespeople and marketing experts is that of adopting the language of your client during the transaction. This principle can be transferred from the commercial sector to the ivory towers of academe. For example, if your examiner customarily uses expressions such as 'an analysis of the assumptions shows . . . ' or 'a critical appraisal of the implications suggests . . . ' or 'the validity of the assertion appears tenuous because . . . ', then use the same sorts of terms and phrases in your responses. Be careful, though, not to take this process too far—merely copying someone else's style is not an automatic recipe for success.

Summarise your argument using the phrasing of the question

At the end of your essay, you should summarise your argument. A helpful way to ensure that you are still on target is to use selected phrases from the question to once again firmly establish in the marker's mind that you have addressed the topic in an organised and cogent way.

Check your essay

Having finished writing your essay, you should briefly re-read it to check for spelling errors and grammatical mistakes. You might also discover ambiguous sentences and phrases which can be quickly remedied. Be certain that you keep your essay neat and legible. The best essay in the class will suffer if it is virtually indecipherable. Remember, your marker is faced with the daunting task of reading many, many essays. Should your essay happen to be in the last pile and also be sloppy and unreadable, imagine how the marker will react.

Attempt every question

Make every attempt to write something, even if you *think* you know nothing about the essay topic. Many students make the mistake of giving up too easily when they strike a question which appears to be beyond their ability or comprehension. The simple truth of the matter is that absolutely no marks whatsoever can be awarded for empty space. Even if you cannot substantiate an argument in an essay with relevant facts and details, list in a logical fashion the major points which you think are most applicable. You might get nothing, but then again perhaps a sympathetic or bleary-eyed and fatigued marker may give you a few marks for your effort. When it comes down to the final tally, a few marks are better than none at all.

Practise your examination essay-writing skills

The emphasis in the preceding section has focused upon being logical in your thinking and organised in your writing. These are very worthwhile qualities to have, but you are probably asking: 'How can I become more logical and more organised in my examination essays, especially under the gaze of the supervisors and the pressure of the clock?'. The answer is, *practise*. If you have had very little prior experience with examinations, try reading the examination papers of past years, especially those written by accomplished students. If past papers are not available to read, try practising your essay-writing skills. Ask a classmate to compose several questions for you. In a spare classroom, write the essays under the same time limits and conditions which you will have in the real examination. Your classmate might help even further by reading your responses and giving you some constructive comments and perhaps even a mark.

THE SHORT-ANSWER EXAMINATION

The short-answer examination can vary from asking you to complete sentences with short phrases to writing several paragraphs on a specific topic. Taking the name of this type of examination literally, the object is to be concise and brief in your responses. If you are asked to write several short paragraphs on a topic, you can generally view the exercise as being a mini-essay. Apply the principles set out in the preceding section, but limit the amount of space you give to examples and illustrative material. The examiner wants to find out what you know, so get straight to the point and don't waffle. Try to use any *buzz words* or important terms and phrases which are basic to the concepts being discussed. You might even underline or highlight these critical words and phrases so they stand out and catch the marker's eye.

THE MULTIPLE-CHOICE EXAMINATION

There has been a very marked increase in the use of multiple-choice examinations in recent years. The popularity of the multiple-choice format is most probably explained by the ease of marking and analysing the results, using computerised answer sheets. Once a collection of questions has been developed, the examiner can sit back and wait for the results print-out. It sounds easy, but the time saved in marking is generally taken up in developing clear and non-ambiguous questions. From the candidate's perspective, multiple-choice questions can cause anxiety, fear—even panic. Most of these candidate reactions are due to faulty preparation. However, even some well-prepared students find the multiple-choice format to be confusing and perplexing. This section will present some guidelines to help you prepare and perform to the best of your ability in multiple-choice examinations.

Preparation

Most candidates who have experienced the rigours of multiple-choice examinations will readily advise that you must know your study material very thoroughly. Unlike the essay format where you might have a choice of questions, and where you can explain your ideas, the multiple-choice examination is far more restrictive and decisive. There is no opportunity for explanation—you are either right, or, you are wrong. No in-betweens exist. However, if there is no penalty for guessing, then choose an answer as you have a one in five chance of getting it right.

Your preparation for multiple-choice examinations is best done on a systematic daily, plus weekly, basis. Plan to go over your notes many times—up to five or six times to have the facts, figures, dates and concepts firmly fixed in your mind. It is not sufficient to be just familiar with your notes; you must know the material well enough to write it down. If you can't write it down, you simply do not know it well enough! For a more detailed discussion about how you can systematise your revision, consult chapters 1 and 8 of this book. In addition to knowing your study material, you will also want to know as much as possible about the examination—number of questions, differential weighting of the examination sections, special conditions, and so on. Ask your lecturer about these examination issues and ask former students who sat for the examination about their experiences.

Starting a multiple-choice examination

If your multiple-choice examination involves a computerised answer sheet, you will initially be asked to complete the candidate identification grid. Consult the section in chapter 9 about how to complete these grids.

The next important step before beginning to answer the questions is to read the directions very carefully. Pay particular attention to the layout of the answer sheet so that you do not commit the very common mistake of recording your answers in the wrong answer spaces. Many students in multiple-choice examinations have found towards the end of the examination that they are one question out—that is, they find that they have been recording, for example, the answer to question 81 in the space for answer 80. Should you discover that this mistake has occurred, summon a supervisor and ask what should be done. You might be offered a chance to re-align the answers after the test booklets have been collected at the end of the examination, but don't count on this concession.

Avoid any transcription errors by checking before recording each and every answer mark.

Working through the examination

In order to do justice to your preparation, there are several guidelines which might be of help to you in multiple-choice examinations:

- Be certain to completely fill in the answer spaces.
- Completely erase any errors.
- Be sure *not* to mark two answers for the same question. The marking machine is generally programmed to automatically mark any such response pattern as wrong.
- At the risk of being repetitious, be certain that you record your answers in the correct answer space.
- Work rapidly, but carefully, through the examination and do the easy questions first.
- Mark the questions you want to reconsider but be careful not to have such a mark confused with an answer.
- Make marginal notes in the test booklet for later consideration.
- Underline key words in the test booklet. Words such as *all, many, some, none, always, sometimes, never, more, less, best* and *least* are some examples of key words which can help you to interpret the questions.

Reconsidering questions and changing answers

The issue of changing answers in multiple-choice tests has been studied carefully. The outcome of these studies suggests that if you have a good reason or a strong hunch that another answer choice is correct, then change it. The results of the studies show that candidates who change answers using these criteria are twice as likely to change an answer from wrong to right as they are to change it from right to wrong.

Guessing

If you have followed the advice of this book, you will have previously determined whether you are penalised for guessing. If there is a built-in penalty system for guessing, then you might be eroding your final mark by guessing the answers to questions about which you are in doubt. On the other hand, if there is no penalty for guessing, you are throwing away a one in five chance of getting a correct answer for every item you leave blank. If you have no intuitive feelings about the question, and all five options appear to be equally plausible (meaning you don't have a clue about the answer!), then you have the problem of selecting between choices (a), (b), (c), (d) and (e). For what it is worth, you might answer (b) to all such questions. The rationale for this choice might be that (a) and (e) are too extreme; (c) is too average; and (b) is closer to the beginning than (d). If you can argue convincingly for another answer choice, then use it.

Cheating

The advent of the multiple-choice examination seems to have promoted the development of exceedingly accurate long-distance visual acuity among examination candidates. What that means in plain English is that multiple-choice candidates have been tempted to read the answer pattern from their neighbour's paper (assuming, of course, that their neighbour is considered to be a brighter and more knowledgeable student).

Examiners have been quick to counter this problem of visual plundering. They have developed parallel versions of the examinations in which the answer sheets are printed in both vertical and horizontal formats in order to deter or confuse would-be cheaters. In addition to these obstacles, there is also the ever-roving supervisor who is observing the head and eye movements of the candidates. Rather than risk a very embarrassing incident and possibly damage your future career, invest your time in a thorough preparation for the examination. Therefore, forget about cheating. Aside from the moral implications of cheating, you might find that your classmates are far less knowledgeable than you.

Checking your answer sheet

Shortly before the end of the examination, save a short amount of time to check your answer sheet to see that you have recorded your answers correctly and fully. Erase any stray marks on your answer sheet, as these could be read by the marking machine as answers. Finally, check to see that you have recorded your candidate identification information correctly.

TRUE–FALSE EXAMINATIONS

As multiple-choice examinations have become more pop-ular, the true–false examination seems to have become less frequently used. Perhaps the explanation is that the mul-tiple-choice examination is really, at core, a true–false examination, but it allows the examiner to assess the knowledge of the candidate more exactingly. In responding to true–false questions, the same principles which were discussed in the previous section can be applied. The candidate should pay particular attention to the wording in the questions and should underline the key words. As there is a 50 per cent chance of guessing correctly in true–false examinations, it is often the case that a penalty (number wrong subtracted from number right) is applied to guessing. Be certain to find out before you start the examination if this is so.

MATCHING QUESTIONS

Matching questions generally appear as two columns of terms and the candidate is asked to match each term with its correct counterpart. When you encounter matching questions, read both columns quickly to obtain an overview of the items. Then consider the items in the left column which you think you know and look down through the right column, searching for the most appropriate match. When you have completed the easy matches, then consider the remainder. If you get stuck, try working in the opposite direction—that is, think first about the remaining items in the right column and look for the most appropriate match in the left column. If you have several unmatched items at the end, guess unless you have been advised not to because of an inbuilt penalty for guessing.

OPEN-BOOK EXAMINATIONS

A recent development in examinations is the open-book approach. With this format, candidates are generally allowed to bring their books and their notes into the examination room. An open-book examination might seem to make examination preparation redundant. Not so. Enticing as the concept might be, the open-book examination requires the candidate to know the material as well as for an orthodox examination. You must know the major topics, their associations and, if necessary, the location in your notes of supporting material. There is generally not sufficient time to go back over notes and books to extract the major ideas and facts during the examination.

The only advantage for the student in an open-book exam is that specific details can be checked. Instead of learning twenty formulae and exhaustive lists of data, know where they can be quickly found in your notes and books. However, be certain that you cover the other material just as thoroughly as you would for a regular examination.

The disadvantage of an open-book examination is that the examiner might expect a higher quality of response because of the concession. Do not be lulled into a *feeling of false confidence* with this format. Prepare just as thoroughly as you would for a regular examination.

LABORATORY EXAMINATIONS

For science-oriented students, laboratory examinations can present challenging assessment experiences. In the medical, engineering, biological and physical sciences, these examinations might take the form of 'musical chairs'. The students are asked to progressively move from specimen to specimen, from microscope to microscope or from one display to the next. The task is generally to identify the tagged or marked part, or perhaps the whole specimen. You may also be asked to answer specific questions, relating to the tagged material. As you have a strict time limit before you have to move on to the next station, the pressure can be extreme.

When preparing for these examinations, you should have thoroughly revised the complete range of your laboratory experiments and all types of relevant laboratory material. It is very important to examine as many different specimens as possible so that you are familiar with the variations which normally occur. When preparing for the examination, move the specimens around so that you are familiar with the different perspectives. Take note of differences in colour, texture, shape and size. The more familiar you are with the specimens in your laboratory group, the better. Study with some classmates and ask them to set up some specimen tests for you. It is important to take note of any unusual features which will distinguish your performance as a superior one.

A few practical suggestions for those students undertaking microscope examinations. Do not touch the slide or specimen under the microscope unless you are allowed to do so. If you think that a specimen has been jarred and the pointer is wrongly positioned, summon a supervisor immediately. If you wear glasses, be certain that they are clean. It's no time to have foggy vision. If you have skipped any places on your answer sheet, be certain that you record your answers in the correct places.

Laboratory practical examinations require many hours of preparation *in the laboratory*. As the laboratory may be open for only a few hours a day, it is very important to prepare and revise on a regular basis throughout the semester. If you leave your revision until the final few days, you may find that there simply is not sufficient time to prepare adequately. You will also find that you have to compete with other students for access to the specimens which you want to examine. It's far better to look upon the final few days as an opportunity to tie up loose ends and consolidate the material in your mind—not the time to organise your first revision visit!

SUMMARY

Examinations vary greatly in format, style, procedures and setting (from large hall to laboratory). Gear your preparation to the type of exam for each subject and, if possible, consult previous candidates and read previous exam papers if they are available. The major goal is to start your revision early so you are sure that you know the topics very well.

Appendix

External secondary education examinations

- Start preparing for your examinations early by collecting information about previous examinations. Having read previous papers and talked to some of last year's candidates, you will recognise examinable topics when they arise during the present year.
- Revise systematically and routinely every week by going over your week's notes. Set aside a regular time for the revision so that it becomes part of your weekly routine. Systematic weekly revision is the best way to deal with examination nerves because *you will know that you know the material* if you have been revising regularly throughout the year.
- If personal discipline is in short supply, arrange to meet a conscientious classmate for these regular revision sessions. Be sure to keep your minds on the appointed task.

- For those students who are starting their revision at a later point in the year, organise a timetable which allows for several revisions of your notes and other materials. Focus upon the major topics on your first revision. Having gone through your notes thoroughly, go through them again, this time picking up the sub-topics and supporting details. If time allows, try to read, recite and write the topics with note headings under each. Being able to write these notes is an acid test of whether you know the material.

- If examination nerves have been a problem for you in the past, consult your school counsellor or a professional psychologist early in the year so that adequate time is available in which to work upon the problem. Read chapter 6 in this book to learn how to relax yourself before your examinations begin.

- Be certain that you get sufficient rest in the weeks preceding your exams. You should be alert and clear thinking during your examination period.

- Your preparation for your examinations should reflect the nature of each subject. You should focus upon problem solving in mathematics and essay writing in humanities subjects. Revise your laboratory exercises in science subjects and be certain that you are knowledgeable about graph interpretation in the social sciences.

- Use the subject syllabus as a general guide for your revision. It is fair to assume that your examinations will reflect the importance of the topics listed in the syllabus.

- Avoid preparing set answers and then writing them out in parrot fashion during the examination. The examiners will quickly recognise essays which do not address the specific issues raised in the questions. Remember, you should demonstrate your ability to interpret the questions, organise your thoughts and write clear, concise and logically argued essays.

- If you are weak in essay writing, start early in the year to improve your skills. Ask your teachers if they would mind reading several mini-essays and giving you some suggestions for improvement. Writing, writing and more writing is the only sure way to improve your essay-writing ability.

- Talk to your teachers and classmates about the differences which you can expect in your examinations. You need to know if it is permissible to use headings in your science subject essays and whether you can use a calculator for problem solving. If calculators are permitted, ask whether it is necessary to show on paper the steps through which the final answer was derived.

- Get organised early and be certain that your revision covers the syllabus adequately. Be aware of your personal examination strengths and weaknesses, and cater for those differences in your revision program. Strengthening your skills and being determined, disciplined and organised in your revision will help to produce a successful outcome.

The medical viva examination

The medical viva examination is a form of assessment used to evaluate the diagnostic and communication skills of medical students and medical graduates who are candidates for specialty memberships or fellowships. The examination usually requires the candidate to examine several patients, one at a time, and then answer questions from a panel of examiners. The following notes have been collected from individuals who have passed the viva examination in a medical course.

- Be certain to have many practise runs with hospital teaching staff before the examination date.

- Practise thinking quickly and clearly by getting together with classmates and testing each other in simulated viva situations.
- Do not assume the absence of positive feedback (or any feedback) from examiners means you are doing poorly. Many examiners approach the examination with practised 'stone' or 'poker' faces.
- Candidates who keep up a stream of constructive commentary maintain control of the examination. Provide relevant information to the examiners (especially in your strong knowledge areas) and do not wait to be asked for further details.
- Do not fabricate tests and procedures if you can't justify their use.
- If you can't respond to a question, say that you don't know and ask if you can go on to another area of questioning.
- If embarrassment is a problem for you, practise becoming embarrassed with classmates who are taking the examiner's role. Learn how to deal with your embarrassment by confronting the problem—don't avoid the issue by pretending it does not exist.
- Establish set routines for examining the chest, abdomen, and so on. Be positive and thorough with the basics, but do not waste the examiner's time by being excessively pedantic.
- Organise your facts and information in a systems approach. Each fact might then bring to mind related facts and issues.
- During ward rounds, do not habitually stand in the back row of the group, hoping to avoid being called upon. Learn by trying and by sometimes making mistakes. Be visible, be willing to have a go, and be prepared to think under pressure.
- Seek help early from clinical staff if you feel that you are at risk of failing.

- Try to anticipate the types of cases you are likely to be given and prepare with a group of classmates.
- If a question is asked which you believe to be ambiguous, ask for clarification or a rephrasing of the question.
- Do not rush into your answers—take time to think the question through and then present a well-organised response.
- If a hasty and incorrect answer has been given, say so straight away, and ask if you can offer a more considered response.
- When you are uncertain about a specific question, start with a general, but relevant point and work towards a more specific answer. While you are giving yourself time to think, be cautious about appearing to waste the examiner's time.
- Do not be alarmed if the examiner appears to be asking a question which is too easy. Go ahead and give the obvious answer.
- Approach the viva examination with the expectation that you will pass. Be positive! Remind yourself about your previous positive performances and accomplishments in academic and non-academic areas and allow the positivism to generalise.
- Start your preparation for your viva examination early. Develop your skills in thinking decisively and logically. Be certain that you know the basics and that you can call up in your mind the necessary lists, characteristics, tests, and so on for the common medical complaints.
- Do not expect to be able to answer every single question in the examination. It is often the case that particularly difficult questions are used in the examination to differentiate the very superior from the superior candidates. The mere mortal candidates who perform at more average levels can be traumatised by these very difficult questions.

- Consider your clothes and present yourself in a professional manner. This is not the time for radical clothing.
- Prepare for your entrance and try to appear as confident and professional as possible. Practise your walk, posture and other important non-verbal communication skills.
- Even though there is a 'performance' element in the viva examination, the important issues for the examiners are whether you know your material well and whether you can use your knowledge in the applied setting. Therefore, the single most important aspect should be preparing your material. Take time each week to revise your work so that you can approach the viva with a confident feeling.

Auditions in the performing arts

- Contact the theatre, agency, school or institution for whom you intend to audition to obtain as early as possible the relevant details (date, time and place of the auditions and the work(s) to be prepared).
- Try to establish who will be auditioning you. What is their background? What are their likes and dislikes? Any information about the judges will help you in your preparation.
- If time permits, talk to friends and colleagues who are established in the relevant field and ask for their advice on your work and audition material.
- Visit the place where your audition is to be held so that you are familiar with the surroundings and any problems posed by the space (for example, a small stage, background noise, poor lighting). Try to accommodate these limitations when rehearsing for your audition.
- Prepare and practise your audition work *very* thoroughly. The more prepared you are, the more relaxed and confident you are likely to be.

- Prior to the audition day, perform your work in front of several knowledgeable friends and experienced colleagues. Ask for detailed and constructive criticism on your performance.
- Make any adjustments to your performance which you think are justified on the basis of the feedback from your friends and colleagues.
- Following your intensive and thorough preparation period, get a good night's rest before the day of the audition. See chapters 6 and 7 on fear control and positive thinking to help overcome excessive nervousness.
- Arrive sufficiently early before your appointed time so that you have plenty of warm-up time. Doing some vigorous exercises can help loosen your body and release nervous tension.
- If, while waiting for your turn, you are watching the performances of those ahead of you, be sure that you are not making unjust comparisons between their performances and your ability. If your mind deviates from positive thinking, hold it in line by saying something like, 'I know my work and I can perform it well!' over and over to yourself.
- Should the jitters and shakes begin to affect you, close your eyes, take a slow and deep breath and then let the air out gently while saying 'relax' to yourself.
- When you are called, pause for a few seconds before getting up. Compose yourself mentally and physically. Another slow, deep breath will be helpful.
- In some auditions, you are likely to be stopped midway through your performance. The comments offered during the interruption might be tactful, but they could also be abrasive. Accept the remarks objectively and do not take any criticism personally.
- If you are unsuccessful in your audition, contact the auditioning authority or agency for an interview a few

days later. Ask for feedback on how you can improve your performance, or your auditioning skills.

Job interview (a form of verbal examination)

- On receiving an appointment for a job interview, telephone the prospective employer to accept the appointment and to confirm the date, time and place of the interview.
- During the telephone call, ascertain, if possible, who the interviewer(s) will be.
- Following the telephone call, start collecting information about the company, the relevant department and the members of the interviewing committee if possible. Obtain, if relevant, the annual reports for the last three years and any other documents pertinent to the firm or department so you can learn about their present activities and future plans. Try to be as informed about the company as your interviewers.
- If you have questions about the job or if you feel you would like to meet the person under whom you will be working, try to arrange a personal interview prior to the date of the scheduled interview. You will probably be more relaxed in a one-to-one situation and hence will be able to create a better impression. Requesting such an interview can also show enthusiasm and keenness.
- Write down questions which you think might be asked during the short list interview. Arrange for a friend to ask these questions under simulated interview conditions and practise your responses. It is important to be able to respond naturally and fluently and not in parrot fashion. See the following checklist for possible interview questions.
    * Why do you want to work for this organisation?
    * How has your background prepared you for the position for which you are applying?

* What other employment possibilities are you presently considering?
* Do you have any special skills and abilities which we should know about?
* How has your academic background prepared you for this particular job?
* Why did you leave your previous job? (If appropriate)
* What characteristics make you a desirable candidate for this job?
* Looking ahead five years, what position do you think you will be filling?
* Should a transfer to a different place be necessary, how do you feel about travelling further each day or perhaps even moving interstate?
* What do you most value in a job?
* Overtime and some weekend work might be necessary. How do you think these arrangements will fit into your personal life?
* What hobbies and interests do you pursue in your free time?
* What personal characteristics are likely to present the greatest difficulty for you, should you be appointed to the position?
* What personal qualities have limited or enhanced your work performance in your previous positions?
* If you were to specify your own salary for this job, how much would you pay yourself?
* If you were a member of this interviewing committee, how would you see yourself as an applicant for the position?
* We've been asking all of the questions so far. Do you have any questions which you would like to ask us?

• Check with friends and job colleagues as to the most appropriate type of clothing to wear to the interview. Hairstyle can also be a concern. Remember, how you present yourself physically is the first communication of the interview. Give careful thought to your appearance.

- Prepare a list of questions to carry into the interview for the inevitable question, 'Do you have any questions which you would like to ask us?'. Consulting your list at this point can show thorough preparation and diligence. If all the pertinent issues have been dealt with, say, 'No, we seem to have covered all of the important points'. Think twice about raising issues about holidays, special leave and sickness benefits which might be misinterpreted by the committee. There is ample time to get these details sorted out after you are offered the job.
- Practise pause responses so that you are not shaken by totally unanticipated questions. Time is on your side and taking a few seconds to think can create an impression of confidence—confidence to remain in control of yourself and the time.
- Practise regaining control over anxiety feelings by taking a slow, deep breath during simulated interviews.
- Practise maintaining appropriate eye contact with all members of the (simulated) interview committee.
- On the day of the interview, be certain to allow time for mishaps and misadventure (tyre puncture, road detours, for example) so that you are not late.
- Have pen and paper with you for any notes which you might want to take.
- Take along some interesting and absorbing reading material so that you do not sit and worry for long periods prior to your interview.
- Before you are called into the interview room, check to see that your hair and clothes are as you want them.
- When called, enter the interview room in a positive and confident fashion. Practise your entrance with a friend and ask for feedback.

- During the interview, do not fall prey to the 'slippery seat syndrome'—that is, do not progressively allow your body to slide into a more prone position, giving an ultra 'laid back' impression. Your body language (eye contact, gestures, posture, facial expressions) is continually communicating important information to your interviewers.
- After the interview, think back over the strong and weak points so that you can improve your 'performance skills' if you are not selected for the position.

Motor vehicle driver's test

- Consult your state driving test authority for information about the driving laws and the driving test.
- Obtain a copy of the driving laws upon which your verbal or written test will be based.
- Study the laws and rules thoroughly.
- Arrange for a driving instructor to teach you the skills of driving. If a family member or friend offers their talent and time, consider their competency, and the insurance cover on their vehicle.
- Generally speaking, it will be cheaper to practise with a friend, but you might be learning their bad habits.
- Practise the driving skills which you will be asked to perform in your test.
- Determine from the state authority whether being tested in an automatic rather than a manual car will place a restriction upon your driver's licence.
- Find an easy and a difficult location in which to practise each driving skill. For example, a three-point turn is easier on a flat wide street than on a hilly narrow street. Practise your skill in reverse parking on flat then hilly streets.
- Practice sessions should initially be carried out in streets with little or no traffic.
- Reward yourself for successfully completing each new skill.

- If you fail in performing a particular driving skill, ask your driving teacher for a step-by-step analysis so you can understand what you did well and not so well.
- Between practice sessions, think through and visualise the integral steps of, for example, a three-point turn. Pretend you are in the driver's seat and go through the steps one by one in your lounge room. At the next practice session in the car, your mind, hands and feet will have the order of events well synchronised.
- Try to preserve and practise your sense of humour. A frayed temper is counterproductive when trying to learn how to drive.
- If you feel yourself getting tense and nervous, take a slow, deep breath and let the air out gently. Say 'relax' to yourself as you exhale.
- On the day of your driving test, keep your mind fruitfully occupied and busy so you don't have time to worry about the test.
- Avoid drinking copious amounts of tea or coffee prior to your test. Too much caffeine (more than two or three cups) can make you feel jittery and will increase the filling rate of your bladder.
- If a worry or negative thought starts, say forcefully to yourself 'STOP!'. Replace the negative thought with a positive one, such as 'I am passing!'.
- If you are a bit nervous when you meet your examiner, tell the person you are nervous. This will not be a new situation to the examiner and talking and perhaps even laughing a bit about the situation will help you feel more comfortable.
- Smoking in a testing car will almost certainly not be allowed.
- If you fail to successfully perform one of the skills during the test, ask the examiner what you did incorrectly. You might be able to try that section of the test again, perhaps in a different location.

- In the event of a total freeze-up of your mind and body, ask the examiner if you can get out of the car for a breath of fresh air and a stretch. Loosening up your body by stretching, shaking your hands, arms, legs and feet will help to release some of the accumulated tension. Take a slow, deep breath and then get back into the car to resume the test.
- During the test, and just prior to one of your difficult manoeuvres, pause for a few moments before beginning the manoeuvre and run through the steps mentally.
- If during stressful conditions you tend to become dry in the mouth, take along some lozenges or a water bottle.
- If the result of your examination is failure, do not let the outcome be a source of depression or confidence erosion. Ask yourself immediately what new aspects you learned from the examination, and plan how these new insights will help you in your next attempt.
- If anxiety and body co-ordination are major problems for you and they have hindered you in passing your driving test(s), consider consulting a professional psychologist. A listing of professionally qualified psychologists can be found in the *Yellow Pages* telephone directory.